Ralph Storer is an experienced and respected climber and walker who has pursued his chosen sports at the highest level. Currently a lecturer in computer studies at Napier University, Edinburgh, one of his great passions is for outdoor activities and the Scottish countryside. He writes regularly for mountaineering and walking magazines and is also the author of *Mountain Trivia Challenge*, *The Joy of Hillwalking*, *Exploring Scottish Hill Tracks* and *100 Best Routes on Scottish Mountains*.

8th April 1999

Ambleside

George Yeomans
01478 650 380
Richard MacClure
01478 613 180

Also by Ralph Storer in Warner Books:

100 BEST ROUTES ON SCOTTISH MOUNTAINS

EXPLORING SCOTTISH HILL TRACKS

50 BEST ROUTES ON SKYE AND RAASEY

Ralph Storer

WARNER BOOKS

A *Warner* Book

First published in Great Britain by David & Charles in 1996
This edition published by Warner Books in 1999

Copyright © Ralph Storer 1996
Maps by Don Sargeant

The moral right of the author has been asserted.

A CIP catalogue record for this book
is available from the British Library.

ISBN 0 7515 2413 1

Typeset by Solidus (Bristol) Limited
Printed and bound in Great Britain by
Clays Ltd, St Ives plc

Warner Books
A Division of
Little, Brown and Company (UK)
Brettenham House
Lancaster Place
London WC2E 7EN

TO THE PEOPLE OF SKYE

Contents

THE CUILLIN

HILL WALKS

COAST WALKS

SHORT WALKS

ISLE OF RAASEY

Acknowledgements

This book is the result of an enduring love affair with the Isle of Skye, nurtured by the many unforgettable days I have spent on the hill, in all weathers and all seasons, with companions too numerous to thank individually. They know who they are and I am ever grateful for their friendship. In particular I would like to thank the members of Dundee University Rucksack Club, with whom I discovered the island on fondly remembered post-exam camping meets. More recently I am indebted to Sue Horsburgh and especially Wendy Gibson, who helped uncomplainingly in the painstaking task of on-the-ground research. Rory Macdonald graciously corrected my attempts at Gaelic pronunciation, although the phonetic guide in the text is solely my responsibility. Don Sargeant turned my amateur sketch maps into works of art.

The content and spirit of this book owe more than I can say to the passion and humour of those who have shared my adventures on the Misty Isle. Long may the glens echo to the thud of their boots.

Introduction

With an area of nearly 700sq miles (1,800sq km), Skye is the second largest of the Hebridean islands lying off the west coast of Scotland. As the eagle flies it is approximately 50 miles (80km) long by 7 to 25 miles (12 to 40km) wide, yet such are the contortions of its shape that the coastline is many hundreds of miles long; so indented is it that on the map the island looks like a group of peninsulas joined together in the middle. No place is more than 5 miles (8km) from the sea, and the nearness of the sea makes walking on Skye a quite different experience from walking in the mainland Highlands.

In broad geographical terms there are five peninsulas radiating from the central part of Skye: Duirinish, Waternish and Trotternish to the north, stocky Minginish to the west and, beyond the old parish of Strath, the fish-tail of Sleat to the south. Most walkers and climbers are attracted to Skye by the Minginish peninsula, for here is to be found the perfect miniature mountain range: the Cuillin, unquestionably the finest mountain range in the British Isles. The gabbro rock of which the Cuillin are largely composed is extraordinarily rough, merciless on skin and clothes but supremely adhesive to feet and other useful parts of the anatomy. The landscape it forms is savage and elemental. There are no hillsides of grass or heather here, no plateau summits; the rock forms vertical faces and narrow ridges, and few summits can be reached without putting hand to rock.

In form, the range consists of a horseshoe-shaped main ridge some 8 miles (13km) long, with satellite ridges radiating out around deep-cut corries. Along this ridge are strung eleven Munros (separate mountains over 914m/3,000ft), nine further Tops (lesser peaks over 914m/3,000ft, as defined in Munro's Tables) and numerous other lower tops, which give the Cuillin skyline a jagged and dramatic appearance when viewed from afar. Mountaineering here is like nowhere else. To climb through a beautiful Cuillin corrie and scramble along the spectacular main ridge from peak to peak through an other-worldly landscape of remarkable rock formations, with island upon island crowding the western horizon

1

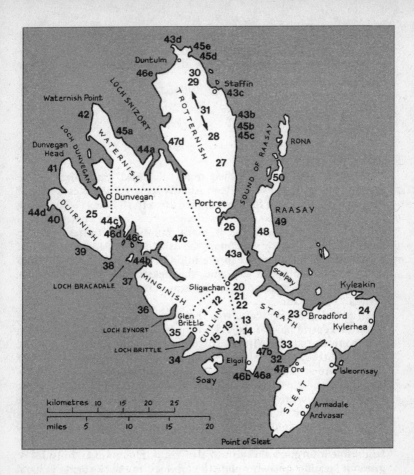

and the whole scene bathed in breathtakingly pure light, is a supreme experience. This book describes nineteen routes in the Cuillin.

Away from the Cuillin there are many other unique and interesting hills to climb, such as the peculiar flat-topped MacLeod's Tables, the crumbling Red Hills and the fantastic pinnacled hills of Trotternish. Twelve routes describe hill walks and scrambles outside the Cuillin.

Encircling the mountains and hills is a coastline that contains the most beautiful, intricate and exciting coastal architecture to be found anywhere in the British Isles. Spectacular sea caves and stacks abound, cliffs soar to over 300m (1,000ft) above Atlantic breakers, and mile upon mile of vertiginous cliff top provides magnificent walks of testing length and remoteness, the equal of any hill walk. Eleven routes describe walks around Skye's coastline.

So well endowed is Skye with fascinating places to explore that many occur only a short distance from the roadside. Five further routes form a compendium of short excursions to places of unusual interest unknown to most Skye tourists, visiting places such as rocky headlands, sea stacks, caves, natural arches, waterfalls and abandoned castles.

Finally, three routes are described on the neighbouring island of Raasay, whose tranquil appearance conceals some seductive hill and coastal scenery and where there are some unexpectedly wild walks.

In all, the walker on Skye and Raasay is spoiled for choice, with a wealth of interesting and exciting walking experiences that are without equal in the British Isles. Add to this the island setting, the magnificent seascapes and the quality of Skye light, and there is something here for everyone, enough for anyone.

Advice on Mountain Walking

The overall difficulty of each route is shown in the form of a grid, as explained on page 9. Many accidents in the Scottish hills are caused by walkers attempting routes outside their capabilities, and the grading system is intended to enable a more realistic route appraisal. All gradings, assessments and descriptions given in the text are for good summer conditions only; in adverse weather, difficulties are compounded and many routes are best avoided. Note also that Cuillin approach paths are notoriously boggy, and after rain become quagmires. Assessments of scrambling difficulty are necessarily subjective, and although great pains have been taken to ensure that gradings are standard across routes, an easy scramble may seem hard to one person and a hard scramble easy to another.

The Cuillin are no place for novice hill walkers. There are few peaks that can be climbed without at least a scramble and there are few easy escape routes. In this three-dimensional labyrinth of rock, route-finding is often a problem, to such an extent that in mist the route onwards may be impossible to locate. The problem is compounded by the magnetic nature of the rock, which makes compass readings dangerously unreliable.

Other problems for the unwary include loose rock and rubble-strewn ledges which necessitate constant vigilance, and sudden atmospheric changes – cloud can seem to appear from nowhere, literally in seconds. In addition, not all Cuillin rock is gabbro. Considerable quantities of basalt have intruded into the gabbro, often in the form of trap-dykes (eroded ladder-like features that sometimes provide an easy route through otherwise difficult terrain). Basalt is much smoother than gabbro and quickly becomes greasy and slippery when wet; great care is required in such conditions, and some routes are best avoided altogether (this is noted in the text where appropriate).

In short, the Cuillin demand great respect and a high level of mountain craft, and they are best tackled in fine weather only. First-timers would do well to seek out the company of someone with Cuillin experience for their initial forays onto the peaks. In an emergency there are public telephones at Sligachan and Glenbrittle Hut, or alert someone local.

In winter the Cuillin have an Alpine attraction, but become serious mountaineering propositions that should be left well alone by walkers. Paths are obliterated by snow, hillsides become treacherous, ridges become corniced, stone shoots become snow gullies, walking becomes more difficult and tiring, terrain becomes featureless in adverse weather, white-outs and spindrift reduce visibility to zero.

Snowfall varies greatly from year to year, but in a normal season the hills get their first dusting of snow in October and winter conditions prevail until after Easter, with pockets of snow lasting into June. No one should venture onto the Cuillin in winter without adequate clothing, an ice-axe, crampons and experience (or the company of an experienced person).

The viability of routes outside the Cuillin in winter depends on grade and conditions; in general, the higher the summer grade the higher the winter grade. Note, however, that even a normally straightforward winter route on a low hill or along the coast may be subject to avalanche or hard ice, to say nothing of potentially life-threatening, severe winter weather.

Map symbols
▲ Munro
△ Top (in Munro's Tables)
● Other summit over 3000′/914m
○ Summit over 2500′/762m
■ Summit over 2000′/610m
□ Summit under 2000′/610m
⊔⊔⊔⊔⊔⊔ Cliff
～～ River
～⊮～ Waterfall
▬▬▬ Ridges

- - - - Route
===== Landrover track
- - - - - Other paths, tracks, etc
===== Road accessible to public
++++++ Railway
++•++ Railway Station
■   Building
⬭ Freshwater Loch
⬛ Sea/Sea Loch

Advice on Coast Walking

Coast walking is not normally regarded as requiring the same degree of fitness, commitment and expertise as mountain walking, yet many Skye coast walks are remote and serious undertakings, with a number of dangers that novice coast walkers will underestimate at their peril. Much of the Skye coastline is distant from the nearest road. Cliffs often overhang, undercut by the sea; their vertiginous edges are often crumbling, honeycombed by rabbits and swept by sudden gusts of wind. There is rarely any shelter from the elements.

Cliff-top terrain is often undulating, requiring constant ascent and descent, sometimes on steep exposed hillsides of grass that become slippery when wet. A different mental attitude from mountain walking is required, as the end point of the walk is hardly ever in view. Cliff-top rivers may cut deep gorges as they fall to the sea, requiring appreciable inland detours to outflank them. In spate, rivers may be dangerous to cross or impassable (this is true all over Skye, on mountain, moor or coast, and rivers spate quickly after rain on Skye). In many places sheep paths at the cliff edge make for excellent going but may also induce a false sense of security, for sheep have small feet and no sense of vertigo; so use their trails with care.

Shoreline coast walks have a different set of dangers from cliff-top coast walks. Shoreline rocks may be greasy, and require care if a twisted ankle or worse is to be avoided. Shoreline crags may be awkward to negotiate. Stonefall, sometimes induced by seabirds, is always a danger at the foot of cliffs. And the greatest danger of all: becoming trapped at the cliff foot by an incoming tide.

In short, as much preparation and care is required for coast walking as for mountain walking. The longer coast walks should be attempted only in dry summer weather in good footwear by well equipped walkers. Heed the warnings in the text. Stay away from dangerous cliff edges. Where a torch is required for the exploration of sea caves, this is noted in the text. Sections of walks that are underwater at high tide and can be undertaken at low tide only are unmistakably marked in the text thus: AT LOW TIDE

ONLY. A tide table is an indispensable item of equipment; tide tables for the west coast of Scotland are obtainable from fishermen's shops on the quayside at Portree.

Sketch Maps

Sketch maps show each route's major features but are not intended for use on the hill. 1:50,000 scale OS maps are adequate for most Skye walks, but OS 1:25,000 Outdoor Leisure Map 8 (OL8) is recommended for the more complex topography of the Cuillin and surrounding areas. Beside each sketch map is indicated the number of the OS map on which the route appears, and the route's starting point and its grid reference.

The classification of mountains as Munros or Tops is based on the 1997 edition of Munro's Tables.

Measurements

Route distances are specified in both miles (to the nearest half-mile) and kilometres (to the nearest kilometre); short distances in the text are specified in metres (an approximate imperial measurement is yards). Mountain heights, specified in metres and feet, have been obtained wherever possible from the latest OS 1:50,000 maps (1992 revision); note that many of these heights, even those of Cuillin Munros, differ from previous editions. The total amount of ascent for the whole route is specified to the nearest 10m (or 50ft) and should be regarded as an approximation only.

Route times (to the nearest half-hour) are based on the time it should take a person of reasonable fitness to complete the route in good summer conditions. They take into account length of route, amount of ascent, technical difficulty, type of terrain and short stoppages, but do not make allowances for long stoppages and adverse weather. They are roughly standard between routes for comparison purposes, and can be adjusted where necessary by a factor appropriate to the individual. In winter, routes will normally take much longer.

Note that river directions, 'left bank' and 'right bank', in accordance with common usage, refer to the direction when facing downstream.

Mountain Names

Most Skye names are of Gaelic or Norse origin, and many are unpronounceable to English-speaking visitors, yet an ability to pronounce them and understand their meaning can add much to the pleasure of walking on Skye. To this end a guide to pronunciation and meaning of mountain names and (where space allows) other physical features is given in the Glossary/Index (p. 112).

The production of such a guide is made difficult by a number of factors, the main one being that OS maps, despite their otherwise excellence, appear to have been named by Sassenachs, for they abound in Gaelic misspellings, misunderstandings, misuses and misplacements. With some misgivings the OS spelling has been retained for purposes of standardisation. Some OS misspellings make pronunciation impossible. In addition, some names have become anglicised to such an extent that it would be pedantic to enforce a purist pronunciation on a non-Gaelic speaker. For example, the correct pronunciation of Ben is something akin to 'Pane', with a soft *n* as in the first syllable of *onion*. Moreover pronunciation differs, sometimes markedly, throughout the Highlands and Islands.

Despite these problems, the phonetic guide given in this book should enable a good attempt at a pronunciation that would be intelligible to a Gaelic speaker. In connection with the guide the following points should be noted:

Y before a vowel is pronounced as in *you*
OW is pronounced as in *town*
CH is pronounced as in Scottish *loch* or German *noch*
TCH is pronounced as *ch* in *church*
OE is pronounced as in French *oeuf* or the *u* in *turn*

Toponymy (the study of place-name meanings) is complicated by OS misspellings, changes in spelling and word usage over the centuries, words with more than one meaning and unknown origin of names (Gaelic, Norse, Irish etc). For example, consider the possible meanings of the names Skye and Cuillin (see Glossary/Index). Meanings given are the most commonly accepted, even if disputed; some names are too obscure to be given any meaning.

Access
There are few access restrictions to the land on Skye, and no stalking restrictions as in the mainland Highlands. The fact that a route is included in this book does not, however, imply a right of way; respect private property, and if in doubt about a path enquire at the nearest house. Please leave the land as you would

7

wish to find it, and in particular do not leave gates open, do not damage farm fences and do not worry livestock. Follow the Country Code.

Grid

	1	2	3	4	5
Grade					●
Terrain			●		
Navigation		●			
Seriousness		●			

Grade
1 Mostly not too steep
2 Appreciable steep sections
3 Some handwork required
4 Easy scramble
5 Hard scramble

Terrain
1 Excellent, often on paths
2 Good
3 Reasonable
4 Rough
5 Tough

Navigation
1 Straightforward
2 Reasonably straightforward
3 Appreciable accuracy required
4 Hard
5 Extremely hard

Seriousness
1 Straightforward escape
2 Reasonably straightforward escape
3 Appreciable seriousness
4 Serious
5 Very serious

An at-a-glance grid for each route indicates the route's overall difficulty, where difficulty consists not only of **grade** (ie technical difficulty) but also type of **terrain** (irrespective of grade), difficulty of **navigation** with a compass in adverse weather, and **seriousness** (ie difficulty of escape in case of curtailment of route for one reason or another. This is based upon a criteria of length and restricted line of escape). These factors vary over the duration of the route and should not be taken as absolute, but they do provide a useful general guide and enable comparisons to be made between routes. Each category is graded, ranging from 1 (easiest) to 5 (hardest).

Route 1: **SGURR NAN GILLEAN**

OS MAP: 32 or OL8
Starting point: Sligachan
(GR: 485298)
Route type: return mountain
scramble
Distance: 7 miles (11km)
Ascent: 1,010m (3,300ft)
Time: 6½ hours

	1	2	3	4	5
Grade					●
Terrain				●	
Navigation					●
Seriousness					●

Assessment: a straightforward approach leads to a hard and exposed final scramble up the south-east ridge on the misleadingly named Tourist Route.

Historical note: the Cuillin remained unclimbed until the physicist and geologist Professor James Forbes persuaded Duncan MacIntyre, a local forester, to guide him up Sgurr nan Gillean, previously considered unclimable, on 7 July 1836. The route they pioneered has since become known as the Tourist Route.

The steep tapering cone of Sgurr nan Gillean at the north end of the Cuillin is one of the most distinctive mountains in the range. For the non-climber there is only one feasible way up: the so-called Tourist Route, but in its latter stages even this is a hard and exposed scramble that requires care and nerve. Should you decide in your wisdom to leave the last few metres for another day, the ascent is still worthwhile for the typically fine Cuillin scenery and views, and Route 2 gives the option of a different way down.

Begin opposite Sligachan Hotel (or just up the road) and take the path along the near bank of the Allt Dearg Mor. At a fork after a few hundred metres, cross the river (bridge) and take another path across the moor to the Allt Dearg Beag, whose beautiful pools and cascades are followed to another fork at another bridge. Cross the bridge and follow the path across the broad flat ridge above Nead na h-Iolaire into heathery Coire Riabhach.

Keeping well above the lochan in the bowl of the corrie, the path climbs steep stony slopes around Sgurr nan Gillean's east face, bears right beneath the towering pinnacles of Pinnacle Ridge and reaches a higher, smaller corrie whose floor is a chaotic jumble of crags and boulders. The path becomes indistinct in places but is well cairned; it continues up the gully at the back of the corrie and reaches the skyline at the foot of the south-east ridge.

Now the excitement begins as the airy crest of the ridge is followed up to the summit platform. There are many route options at first, but as the steepening summit cone gets nearer the scrambling becomes

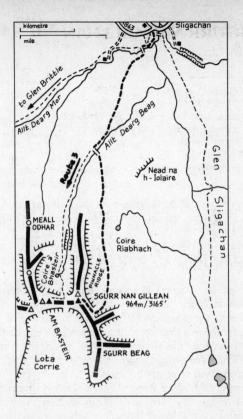

harder and more exposed. On the last 30m/100ft there are only two possible routes: the extremely narrow crest of the ridge, or sloping rocks to the left. It is at this point that those of a nervous disposition may not wish to proceed, and remember that it will be necessary to descend the same way.

The final few metres along the narrow summit ridge are very exposed, especially at a short hiatus where parts of the anatomy other than hands and feet are likely to be put to good use. The summit itself is an eerie platform from which none of the supporting ridges can be seen, as if it were suspended in the sky. By scrambling just beyond the summit, views of the west ridge and magnificent Pinnacle Ridge can be obtained.

Unless you decide to take up permanent residence on the summit, the only way down for non-climbers is via Harta Corrie (see Route 2) or the way you came up.

11

Route 2: **SGURR BEAG AND SGURR NA H-UAMHA**

OS MAP: 32
Starting point: Sligachan (via Sgurr nan Gillean) (GR: 485298)
Route type: add-on mountain scramble to Route 1 (distance/ascent/time include ascent of Sgurr nan Gillean)
Distance: 11 miles (18km)
Ascent: 1,160m (3,800ft)
Time: 9 hours

	1	2	3	4	5
Grade					●
Terrain				●	
Navigation					●
Seriousness					●

Assessment: an entertaining scramble on the 'last nail' in the Cuillin horseshoe, and a descent amid imposing rock scenery on the hidden east side of the range.

Historical note: Sgurr na h-Uamha was first climbed by Charles Pilkington's party in 1887, via a crack that gave 'a capital scramble'.

The two minor peaks of Sgurr Beag and Sgurr na h-Uamha, hidden from view behind Sgurr nan Gillean in the famous view from Sligachan, complete the north end of the Cuillin horseshoe. Sgurr na h-Uamha in particular is a fine little mountain whose exciting ascent is of a similar standard to the final section of the Sgurr nan Gillean Tourist Route. They are unjustly ignored by 'tourists' but lie only a short distance away and offer good views of the main peak.

The stony summit of Sgurr Beag is only a short walk from the foot of the south-east ridge of Sgurr nan Gillean and easy slopes of grass and stones descend from it to the Bealach a' Ghlas-choire below Sgurr na h-Uamha. Beyond the bealach the beautiful conical peak of Sgurr na h-Uamha forms a fitting 'last nail' in the Cuillin horseshoe. From all other approaches its ascent involves rock climbing, and even from Sgurr Beag the two-tiered north ridge that rises from the bealach looks extremely sharp. On closer inspection, however, the first tier provides lovely easy scrambling on satisfying gabbro blocks, with little exposure. The second tier is hard but handholds are excellent; the route goes initially left, then back right and straight up the centre of the face towering overhead. As on the final scramble up Sgurr nan Gillean, this second tier should be attempted by experienced scramblers only, who should remain aware that they will have to reverse it.

A descent westwards from the Bealach a' Ghlas-choire into the remote fastness of Harta Corrie provides a way back to Sligachan through some of the wilder and less trodden parts of the Cuillin. Steep broken slopes lead down into Lota Corrie, a small crag-girt bowl

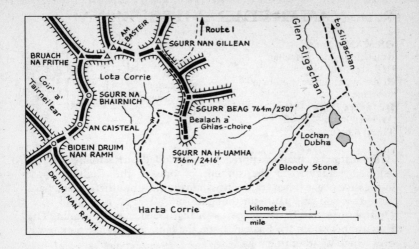

hemmed in by the peaks of the northern Cuillin. A tremendous water chute, the longest in the Cuillin, falls from here into upper Harta Corrie. The route down keeps to its left and is cairned.

Upper Harta Corrie is an impressive spot beneath the eastern buttresses of An Caisteal, whose huge walls of rock, over 300m/1,000ft high, hang above the corrie like curtains. A further short descent leads to the lower corrie, a deep U-shaped trench that curves around the rocky flanks of Sgurr na h-Uamha to meet Glen Sligachan. A path is picked up on the right bank of the river and this leads past the Bloody Stone in the mouth of the corrie. The Bloody Stone is a curious, isolated boulder, some 10m (30ft) high, around which were piled the bodies of MacLeods and MacDonalds after yet another bloody battle between those feuding clans on yet another godforsaken patch of remote moorland. The path eventually joins the Glen Sligachan path, which leads back to Sligachan.

Route 3: **AM BASTEIR**

OS MAP: 32 or OL8
Starting point: Sligachan
(GR: 485298)
Route type: return mountain
scramble
Distance: 7 miles (11km)
Ascent: 930m (3,050ft)
Time: 6 hours

	1	2	3	4	5
Grade					●
Terrain				●	
Navigation					●
Seriousness					●

Assessment: a complex approach to a secluded corrie, followed by an exposed scramble to the summit of one of the Cuillin's most impressive peaks. The scrambling is mostly easy, but there is one hard move that will give pause for thought.
Dental note: Am Basteir gets its evocative Gaelic name (meaning The Executioner) from the Basteir Tooth, the fantastic axe-like rock tower over which its summit hangs.

West of Sgurr nan Gillean the main Cuillin ridge and its satellites enclose secluded Coire a' Bhasteir to form one of the most majestic skylines on Skye. At the back of the corrie the main ridge rises steeply from the Bealach a' Bhasteir to form the east ridge of Am Basteir, and then falls away vertically to the dramatic Basteir Tooth. The east ridge of Am Basteir is a hard but engrossing scramble, and for non-climbers it is the only way to the summit of this most impressive rock peak.

From Sligachan follow the Sgurr nan Gillean Tourist Route (see Route 1) as far as the fork at the bridge over the Allt Dearg Beag; then instead of going left across the bridge, continue up the left bank (right side) of the river towards Coire a' Bhasteir. On approaching the corrie, the stream flows through a gorge whose high rock walls merge on the right into slabs at the foot of the north-east ridge of Sgurr a' Bhasteir. A cairned route through the slabs climbs high above the gorge, cutting across the shoulder of the ridge. There are one or two places where easy, slightly exposed scrambling is required, and it is important not to lose the line of cairns in mist. On exit from the gorge, two cairned lines lead into the bowl of the corrie, one beside the river and one higher up.

A secret lochan lies deep in the heart of the corrie. A path crosses the stream at its outflow, outflanks the band of crags at the back of the corrie on the left and reaches the foot of the summit cliffs of Am Basteir, which tower menacingly overhead. Climb the boulder ruckle to their left to reach the Bealach a' Bhasteir, where you will want to pause to survey the east ridge that rears dauntingly skywards in front of you. With one exception, its ascent surprisingly involves mostly

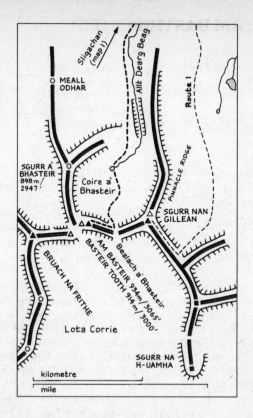

walking and easy scrambling along a narrow exposed crest, with any hard sections easily bypassed on ledges on the Lota Coire side (beware loose rubble on these ledges).

The 'one exception' is an unavoidable obstacle that has turned back many a hopeful scrambler: a 3m (10ft) vertical rib directly on the crest about two-thirds of the way up. On ascent this rib must be descended by facing inwards, lowering yourself from step to step; it is hard, but there are good jug-handles, and these make it easier to haul yourself up on the return. Once the rib has been negotiated, the small summit platform is soon reached without further ado.

Beyond the summit it is possible to continue a short distance to the top of the western cliffs, to view the top of the Basteir Tooth. This involves a hard scramble down a wall and across a slab, easier on the way back. The only descent route from Am Basteir, unless you can abseil, is the way you came up.

15

Route 4: **BRUACH NA FRITHE**

OS MAP: 32 or OL8
Starting point: head of Glen Brittle
(GR: 424258)
Route type: circular mountain
scramble
Distance: 6¹/₂ miles (11km)
Ascent: 890m (2,900ft)
Time: 6 hours

	1	2	3	4	5
Grade				●	
Terrain			●		
Navigation					●
Seriousness			●		

Assessment: an easy scramble up a shattered ridge to one of the best viewpoints in the Cuillin, with a number of route options that pass through stunning rock scenery.

Non-scramblers' note: an ascent via Fionn Coire is one of the easiest ascents to the summit of a Cuillin Munro and provides a good introduction to Cuillin rock scenery; however, it is still necessary to take care and to keep an eye on the weather.

When climbed via Fionn Coire, Bruach na Frithe is one of the easiest mountains in the Cuillin. The view from the summit is one of the finest in the range, with the savage rock peaks around Coire a' Bhasteir cleaving the sky in Dolomitic splendour. Of the several routes to the summit, the narrow shattered north-west ridge offers the most exhilarating ascent, but note that the rock is basalt and becomes slippery when wet. In its lower reaches the ridge divides into two spurs, and the shallow basin between them, drained by the Allt Mor an Fhinn Choire, contains the most featureless terrain in the Cuillin.

A time-honoured path between Sligachan and the head of Glen Brittle crosses the Bealach a' Mhaim at the foot of the ridge and gives easy access from either starting point; the Glen Brittle approach is the shorter. From the lochan on the bealach, climb the nearer (more westerly) of the two spurs. Grassy slopes lead up over a couple of levellings and then stonier slopes climb more steeply to the point where the two spurs join. The ridge then quickly narrows and soon the scrambling begins. The scrambling is in the easy-to-moderate category; the crest of the ridge has some hard moves, but there is always an easier line to the right. The hardest section is where the ridge rears up steeply about half-way along, and there is some exposure here. A bypass path on the south-west face can be used to avoid this steepening, but take care not to wander out along rubble-strewn ledges to dead-ends.

To descend from the summit, go down the stony east ridge to the gap between Bruach na Frithe and Sgurr a' Fionn Choire. Beyond the gap the rock bastion of Sgurr a' Fionn Choire blocks the way onward,

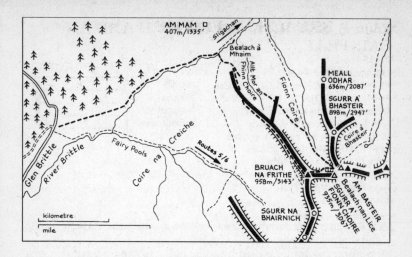

but fortunately there is an easy traverse path that contours around it to the Bealach nan Lice. From the bealach it is worth wandering out along the south ridge of Sgurr a' Bhasteir immediately beyond to study Pinnacle Ridge of Sgurr nan Gillean and the spectacular Basteir Tooth below Am Basteir. The route down descends slopes of boulders and scree from the bealach into Fionn Coire, an untypically grassy but charming Cuillin corrie with an attractive shelf of small lochans. Once into the bowl of the corrie, cross into the basin between the two spurs of the north-west ridge and regain the Bealach a' Mhaim.

Note: from near the Bealach nan Lice, scree slopes also descend into Coire a' Bhasteir, providing an interesting route back to Sligachan that involves slightly more scrambling (see Route 3). Note also the add-on scramble provided by Route 5.

Route 5: **SGURR A' BHAIRNICH AND AN CAISTEAL**

OS MAP: 32 or OL8
Starting point: head of Glen Brittle (via Bruach na Frithe) (GR: 424258)
Route type: add-on mountain scramble to Route 4 (distance/ascent/time are for round trip from head of Glen Brittle, including ascent of Bruach na Frithe)
Distance: 6½ miles (11km)
Ascent: 980m (3,200ft)
Time: 7 hours

	1	2	3	4	5
Grade					●
Terrain					●
Navigation					●
Seriousness					●

Assessment: a sensational scramble that includes the traverse of one of the sharpest summits in the Cuillin.
Map note: do not be misled by some old maps and guidebooks that transposed the names of Coir' a' Tairneilear and Coir' a' Mhadaidh.

South of Bruach na Frithe, the main Cuillin ridge crosses the two minor peaks of Sgurr na Bhairnich and An Caisteal, and their thrilling traverse is described here as an optional add-on to the ascent of Bruach na Frithe (Route 4).

The route begins with the descent of Bruach na Frithe's south ridge, which is easy but quite narrow, with one or two short scrambles that can be awkward when wet. Sgurr na Bhairnich, the next top along, is easily reached by a short ascent; some moderate moves on the crest can be easily avoided on the right. A steep descent on rubble-strewn ledges then leads down to the deep cleft between Sgurr na Bhairnich and An Caisteal. A short distance down, a 5m (16ft) vertical descent to the head of a gully can be bypassed on the left, after which it is best to keep left and hold to the steeply descending crest; ledges on the right look more tempting initially but become awkward lower down.

From the cleft An Caisteal rears up in such an improbable fashion that most scramblers will rightly think twice before tackling it; fortunately a stony gully provides an easy descent to Coir' a' Tairneilear if necessary. The ascent begins with a polished vertical wall whose holds force you off balance, and only those who are sure of their ability should attempt it. Above the wall there are no comparable difficulties; the route veers left until beneath the imposing summit buttress, then regains the crest of the ridge by a gully on the right. The final section to the summit, which looks impossibly sharp and exposed from Sgurr na Bhairnich, turns out to be a short stroll along a sensational path.

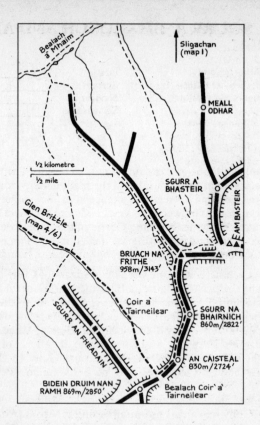

The descent of the far side of An Caisteal to the Bealach Coir' a' Tairneilear is mostly a moderate scramble, but it too has its moments. First, a couple of notches must be negotiated; the first can be avoided on rubble-strewn ledges to the left, the second by a path a few metres down on the right. Then the ridge continues, narrow but easy, until a vertical knob of rock blocks the way to the bealach. This can be bypassed by an exposed but easy traverse along a ledge on the left or by descending to easier slopes on the right.

To the south of the Bealach Coir' a' Tairneilear the attractive summit of Bidein Druim nan Ramh is a no-go area for non-climbers, so leave the ridge at the bealach to descend scree slopes into Coir' a' Tairneilear; cairns indicate the best line if you can find them. Once into the corrie, a path follows the right bank of the river all the way down to Coire na Creiche and Glen Brittle.

Route 6: **SGURR AN FHEADAIN**

OS MAP: 32 or OL8
Starting point: head of
Glen Brittle (GR: 424258)
Route type: circular mountain
scramble
Distance: 5½ miles (9km)
Ascent: 640m (2,100ft)
Time: 5½ hours

	1	2	3	4	5
Grade					●
Terrain					●
Navigation					●
Seriousness				●	

Assessment: a unique and exciting scramble beside 'The Waterpipe' on a basalt peak that thrusts out from the main Cuillin ridge.

Battle note: Coire na Crèiche has a place in history as the site of the last battle ever fought between the MacLeods and the MacDonalds, in 1601. The corrie's name (meaning Corrie of the Spoils) derives from the division of the spoils following the defeat of the MacLeods.

South of Bruach na Frithe, the wide open spaces of Coire na Creiche are backed by the peaks of Sgurr na Bhairnich, An Caisteal and Bidein Druim nan Ramh. From Bidein a short spur juts out to the imposing pyramid-shaped peak of Sgurr an Fheadain to divide the upper corrie into two: Coir' a'Tairneilear to the north and Coir' a' Mhadaidh to the south. Sgurr an Fheadain soars above the flat floor of Coire na Creiche, its face split by the deep Waterpipe Gully (a classic Very Severe rock climb) that gives the peak its name (Peak of the Waterpipe).

An ascent via the exciting north-west spur to the left of Waterpipe Gully has a real mountaineering feel to it. Although the scrambling is no more than moderate if the crest is adhered to, the route rises through some spectacular rock scenery and gives a fine sense of achievement. It should be undertaken by experienced scramblers only, as the rock is often loose and the exposure above Waterpipe Gully is considerable; note also that the rock is mainly basalt and should be left well alone when wet. Beyond the summit a continuing scramble along the south-east ridge enables a fine circuit to be made.

The foot of the peak is reached by a path that descends from the head of Glen Brittle to the River Brittle and continues up the riverbank into Coire na Creiche. After half an hour it passes the Fairy Pools, a series of waterfalls and rock pools that form perhaps the finest stretch of streamway in the Cuillin. At the foot of Sgurr an Fheadain, to the left of the lowest point, a broad grassy rake pushes up into the cliffs, and the scrambling begins on slabs to the left of this. Once above the slabs, aim right to gain the north-west spur and then climb skywards.

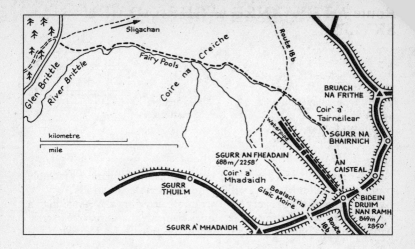

There are numerous choices of route and the excitement increases as height is gained.

Once over the summit, a rock buttress is outflanked by an easy scramble on the right to reach a small bealach. Another easy scramble then leads up to a shattered ridge that provides a pleasant stroll to the saddle below Bidein Druim nan Ramh. From here, descend either into Coir' a' Tairneilear or Coir' a' Mhadaidh. The slopes of scree and rubble falling into Coir' a' Tairneilear provide much the easier way down, but Coir' a' Mhadaidh is the more attractive corrie if you can find the route down into it. The key to the Coir' a' Mhadaidh descent is an awkward stone shoot (cairned at the top) at the near end of a grassy terrace that descends diagonally from the Bealach na Glaic Moire. The route is described in Route 18b.

OS MAP: 32 or OL8
Starting point: Glen Brittle
Youth Hostel (GR: 409225)
Route type: circular mountain
scramble
Distance: 6 miles (10km)
Ascent: 1,340m (4,400ft)
Time: 8½ hours

	1	2	3	4	5
Grade					●
Terrain					●
Navigation					●
Seriousness					●

Assessment: a long, hard and continuously stimulating scramble over three Cuillin Munros, with some memorable situations.

Scrambling note: the very hard scramble up Sgurr a' Mhadaidh can be avoided by traversing scree slopes beneath the cliffs of Sgurr a' Mhadaidh and climbing a prominent scree gully to An Dorus.

Coire a' Ghreadaidh is a beautiful corrie whose pools and waterslides can be irresistibly inviting on a hot day. Moreover, the corrie headwall is formed by three massive Munros whose traverse provides a skyline scramble that is one of the most continuously exciting in the Cuillin.

Begin at Glen Brittle Youth Hostel and take the path up the left bank (right side) of the tumbling burn to reach the flat bowl of the corrie and the picturesque waterslides at its back. From here, climb directly up steep, tedious slopes of grass and scree to the saddle seen above on the summit ridge of Sgurr Thuilm, an outlying top on the northern corrie rim.

From the summit of Sgurr Thuilm, descend the gentle south-east ridge to where it abuts sharply against the side of Sgurr a' Mhadaidh. The scramble up Sgurr a' Mhadaidh attacks the left of two rock ribs and is hard and exposed. An initial very steep section is bypassed on the right, and then there is an adrenalin-pumping section on the crest before an easier line can again be taken on the right. Higher up, a cairn marks the start of a path that traverses right to avoid the summit crags, which are for rock climbers only, and then an easy scramble leads to the narrow summit crest.

Heading southwards around the corrie, bouldery slopes lead down to a moderate scramble into and out of the gap in the ridge known as An Dorus (The Door), and then it is mainly a walk to another cleft in the ridge called the Eag Dubh (Black Cleft). Next comes a hard, slabby scramble up to the Wart, a rock bastion that is easily bypassed on the right to gain the summit of Sgurr a' Ghreadaidh.

Beyond the summit the ridge narrows in spectacular fashion over Sgurr a' Ghreadaidh's south top, and descends to a bealach; the

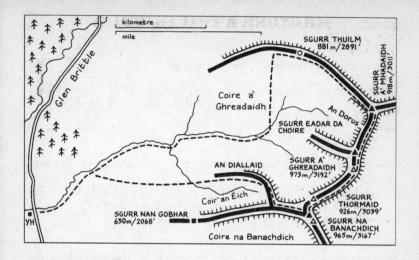

scrambling is continuously hard, dramatic and totally absorbing. Impressive-looking Sgurr Thormaid, with its three 'teeth', rears beyond the bealach, but for once the scrambling turns out to be relatively easy; the easiest line keeps to the left on the way up and to the right on the descent of the far side. The final ascent of the day, up Sgurr na Banachdich, is also easy.

From the summit of Sgurr na Banachdich numerous cairned lines descend the mountain's stony western slopes to a small plateau at the junction of the west ridge and the spur ridge leading to An Diallaid. Descend over An Diallaid or down Coir' an Eich between the two ridges, then head straight down across the moor to rejoin the outward route. Alternatively, continue out along the west ridge to Sgurr nan Gobhar (see Route 8).

Route 8: **SGURR NA BANACHDICH**

OS MAP: 32 or OL8
Starting point: Glen Brittle Hut
(GR: 411216)
Route type: circular mountain
scramble
Distance: 6 miles (10km)
Ascent: 1,010m (3,300ft)
Time: 6 hours

	1	2	3	4	5
Grade					●
Terrain					●
Navigation					●
Seriousness				●	

Assessment: a sensational scramble over rocky towers on the main Cuillin crest.

Waterfall note: the ascent route passes the longest waterfall in the Cuillin, the Eas Mor, which plunges 24m (80ft) into an enormous open gorge at the foot of Coire na Banachdich.

Sgurr na Banachdich ranks alongside Bruach na Frithe as one of the easiest of all Cuillin peaks when ascended via An Diallaid (see Route 7), but the most interesting circuit on the peak combines two scrambling routes from Glen Brittle: via Coire na Banachdich and the south-east ridge, and via Sgurr nan Gobhar and the west ridge.

Coire na Banachdich is a large, open corrie that provides an easy approach to the Bealach na Banachdich, the low point on the corrie headwall at the foot of the south-east ridge. The main path into the corrie begins at Glen Brittle Hut and crosses the Allt Coire na Banachdich at a pipeline to reach the gorge of the Eas Mor. At the head of the gorge the path forks: take the left branch up into the corrie and around the foot of Window Buttress (the spur on the right) to reach a fine gorge on the right at the foot of the headwall. To outflank the headwall crags, follow a cairned line that veers right, up easy slabs on the left side of the gorge, then traverses back left across a broad bouldery shelf to the bealach.

The south-east ridge rises from the bealach and begins as an easy walk on shattered rock over a subsidiary top. The rock then improves over a second top to provide sensational scrambling. This second top can be bypassed on the left, but good routefinding is required if you are not to lose the path and get into difficulties on rubble-strewn ledges. The ascent of the second top begins with a difficult section (bypassable on the left), and higher up there is a narrow rib of large blocks that require dramatic step-ups. On the descent of the far side, the only hard section is a short wall near the foot, which is steep but has good holds. From the gap beyond the second top a shattered crest continues more easily to the summit of Sgurr na Banachdich.

From the summit, descend southwards to the small plateau at the

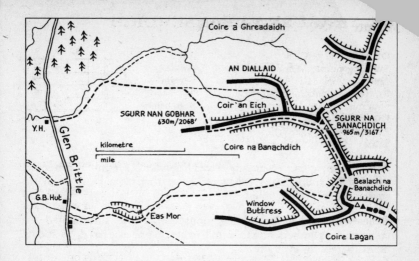

junction of the west ridge and the An Diallaid spur, as for Route 7, then keep straight on to follow the west ridge out to Sgurr nan Gobhar. The ridge is narrow and offers an enjoyable mixture of walking and easy scrambling, and Sgurr nan Gobhar is a fine eyrie overlooking Glen Brittle. The quickest route down to the glen is a stone shoot (steep, earthy and requiring care at the top) that descends into Coire a' Ghreadaidh from the small saddle between Sgurr nan Gobhar's twin tops. From its foot, cross the moor to the path beside the Allt a' Choire Ghreadaidh, reaching the roadside a few minutes' walk from your starting point.

9: SGURR DEARG

MAP: 32 or OL8
Starting point: Glen Brittle campsite (GR: 414205)
Route type: circular mountain scramble
Distance: 5 miles (8km)
Ascent: 990m (3,250ft)
Time: 6 hours

	1	2	3	4	5
Grade				●	
Terrain					●
Navigation					●
Seriousness					●

Assessment: an essentially straightforward scramble rendered exciting by tremendous exposure and perhaps the most dramatic surroundings in the Cuillin.

'Inaccessible as it looks, this pinnacle may be surmounted by experienced climbers who love to do what no one else has done and to boast thereof for ever after.'

> J.A. MACCULLOCH on the 'Inaccessible Pinnacle'
> (*The Misty Isle of Skye*, 1905)

The round of Coire Lagan is a long-standing scramblers' test piece. It develops into what is technically a rock climb, but the ascent of Sgurr Dearg, which begins the round, involves no hard scrambling and provides a route through perhaps the most spectacular situations in a mountain range full of spectacular situations.

From Glen Brittle campsite take the path (of sorts) that begins behind the toilet block and makes a rising traverse left across the moor to the Allt a' Mhuilinn. The path follows this stream, crosses another path, and climbs to a conspicuous cairn-shaped boulder at the foot of the south-west shoulder of Sgurr Dearg. The stony, well trodden route up the shoulder begins steeply and then eases off to reach a narrow section of ridge just below the summit, where the scrambling is slightly exposed but no more than moderate.

The summit is a short sharp arête that is one of the most awesome spots on the Cuillin ridge, for looming even higher is the preposterous blade of rock known as the Inaccessible Pinnacle. This mighty monolith teeters some 24m (80ft) above the south-east slopes of Sgurr Dearg, overtopping the summit by about 8m (25ft) to form the only Munro that requires a rock climb for its ascent. Its sensational situation above abysmal drops on each side has been known to cause more than one normally rock-steady ridge wanderer to hug the ground for confirmation of its solidity. Climbers undertaking the round of the Coire Lagan skyline will ascend the facing (west) ridge of the 'In Pin' (a Difficult rock climb) and descend its far (east) ridge (a Moderate

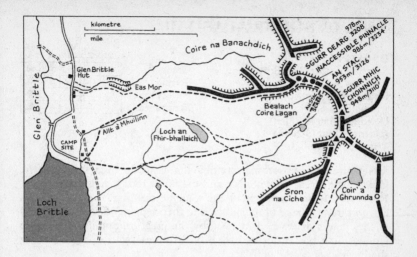

rock climb) but, fortunately for others, it can be bypassed by a broad ramp at its base on the Coire Lagan side.

Descend rough ground to the neck of rock between Sgurr Dearg and the 'In Pin', with vertiginous drops left to Coruisk, and follow the ramp round to the foot of the pinnacle's east ridge. The going hardly constitutes a scramble, yet the situation and the occasional rubble on the ramp cause most walkers to negotiate this section in a less-than-upright posture.

From the foot of the east ridge it is worth scrambling up to the summit of An Stac for its unrivalled view of the In Pin, but the scramble should then be reversed to regain the ramp, as the continuation eastwards from the summit of An Stac is a Difficult rock climb. Continue down the broad undercut ramp as it traverses beneath the crest of An Stac. Take care to continue left around a corner (cairn), rather than right down some tempting scree that leads to crags, and regain the crest of the ridge at the Bealach Coire Lagan.

The scramble up Sgurr Mhic Choinnich, the next peak on the ridge, along perhaps the sharpest crest in the Cuillin, can be explored by those who are not of a nervous disposition, but the corrie skyline eventually becomes the preserve of rock climbers. From the Bealach Coire Lagan, descend scree slopes (An Stac Screes) to the heart of Coire Lagan, a beautifully glaciated corrie, wonderfully wild and rocky, in whose upper bowl a lovely lochan nestles among enormous boiler-plate slabs. The path down to Glen Brittle descends from the right-hand corner of the lochan. It is a pleasant descent across the moor, with the climber's playground of Sron na Ciche cliffs to your left and in front of you the endless sea.

27

Route 10: **SGURR ALASDAIR**

OS MAP: 32 or OL8
Starting point: Glen Brittle campsite
(GR: 414205)
Route type: circular mountain
scramble
Distance: 5 miles (8km)
Ascent: 970m (3,200ft)
Time: 6½ hours

	1	2	3	4	5
Grade					●
Terrain					●
Navigation					●
Seriousness					●

Assessment: an absorbing scramble that visits the highest peak in the Cuillin, the Great Stone Shoot and the finest rock face in Britain.
Rock note: the route passes the Cioch (meaning 'the Breast'), an extraordinary wodge of rock affixed to the mighty cliff face of Sron na Ciche. It was discovered in 1906 by the great mountaineer Norman Collie, after his curiosity had been aroused by the large evening shadow it cast on the cliff face.

Coire Lagan is bounded on its south side by a branch ridge that runs over Sgurr Alasdair, Sgurr Sgumain and Sron na Ciche. Sgurr Alasdair is a beautiful pointed peak that makes a fitting highest Cuillin, even though its summit is composed of basalt rather than gabbro. For non-climbers there are only two routes to the top: via the south-west ridge from Sgurr Sgumain and via the Great Stone Shoot; the former is better for ascent, the latter for descent.

From Glen Brittle campsite follow the Coire Lagan path, which climbs from behind the toilet block onto the moor. Above Loch an Fhir-bhallaich, branch right at a fork to the foot of the imposing cliff face of Sron na Ciche, a remarkable wall of contorted gabbro that towers 300m (1,000ft) overhead. The route to Sgurr Sgumain ascends the Sgumain Stone Shoot beside the cliffs to the Bealach Coir' a' Ghrunnda. About two-thirds of the way up, there are some enormous boulders that form a cave, and hidden on the cliff face to the right of these is the Cioch. The Cioch and the great slab to which it clings can be viewed by a short, moderate scramble that goes diagonally right up a shelf from the foot of the boulders.

From the Bealach Coir' a' Ghrunnda a path climbs easily to the bouldery summit of Sgurr Sgumain; but reaching the Sgumain–Alasdair bealach from here is not so easy. An immediate short sharp scramble up an exposed rib of rock leads to a narrow ridge that ends in a steep drop to the bealach, avoidable by an easy scramble on either side. Alternatively, leave the crest of the ridge at the beginning of the rib and descend ledges on the Coire Lagan side to reach a path that traverses to the bealach.

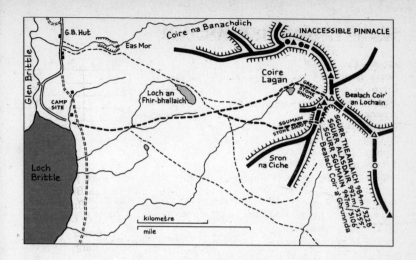

A *gendarme* on the bealach is bypassed on the right by a path that leads away from a *mauvais pas* (a 4m/13ft wall) on the crest of Sgurr Alasdair's towering south-west ridge to a not surprisingly well-worn chimney further right. The chimney is a hard scramble but the holds are good. Above it, pick a route with care up the steep and shattered summit slopes, trending back left to the crest to reach the airy summit.

An easy but somewhat exposed scramble leads down to the gap between Sgurr Alasdair and Sgurr Thearlaich, and from here the Great Stone Shoot descends into Coire Lagan. At one time its 400m/1,300ft of scree provided the fastest descent in the Cuillin, but its upper section is now very steep and bare and requires care. Once down into the corrie, pick up the Glen Brittle path on the right side of the lochan.

Route 11: **SGURR DUBH MOR**

OS MAP: 32 or OL8
Starting point: Glen Brittle
campsite (GR: 414205)
Route type: circular mountain
scramble
Distance: 6 miles (10km)
Ascent: 970m (3,200ft)
Time: 7 hours for return route
1 below; add 1½ hours for a 2a
and 2b, and 3 hours for 2c

	1	2	3	4	5
Grade					●
Terrain					●
Navigation					●
Seriousness				●	

Assessment: a beautiful secret corrie and a sharp peak hidden beyond its headwall combine to produce one of the most stunning of all Cuillin scrambles.

Possible return routes: (1) descend Coir' a' Ghrunnda; (2) traverse beneath the Alasdair–Thearlaich cliffs to the Bealach Coir' a' Ghrunnda and (a) descend the Sgumain Stone Shoot (see Route 10), (b) descend along the cliff top of Sron na Ciche, or (c) climb Sgurr Alasdair and descend the Great Stone Shoot (see Route 10).

Coir' a' Ghrunnda is at the same time the wildest and most beautiful of all Cuillin corries. Its sandy-shored lochan, hemmed in by high peaks, the barrier of vast boiler-plate slabs that guard its entrance and the incredibly rough rocks at the back of the corrie are all without equal. And behind the corrie headwall lies the hidden Munro of Sgurr Dubh Mor, which has one of the sharpest summits in the range.

From Glen Brittle campsite, take the Coire Lagan path as far as the first stream, then cross to another path that continues across the moor past the Allt Coire Lagan. Keep going until you get close to a conspicuous boulder perched on the hillside above left, then head uphill past the boulder to join a higher path that traverses in from Coire Lagan. This rounds the south-west shoulder of Sron na Ciche into the trough of lower Coir' a' Ghrunnda and climbs the corrie high up on the left, avoiding the immense boiler plates in the centre. The path climbs to the nick in the skyline from which the Allt Coir' a' Ghrunnda tumbles; the waterfall is outflanked on the left by an easy scramble. Over the skyline you emerge into the secret bowl of the upper corrie, with its idyllic lochan.

The most interesting route up to the main ridge climbs to the gap between Sgurr Dubh na Da Bheinn and Caisteal a' Garbh-choire, reaching the skyline through a window formed by a leaning slab. The ascent involves some delightful, easy scrambling on a staircase of large boulders that are the roughest in the Cuillin; the rock is peridotite, famously described by an early guidebook as 'painfully adhesive'.

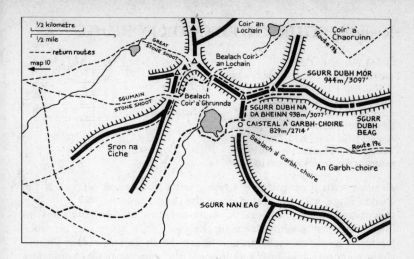

From the gap, easier slopes lead to the broken but shapely summit of Sgurr Dubh na Da Bheinn.

Leave the main ridge here for a side ridge to Sgurr Dubh Mor. The short descent to the saddle between the two peaks is easy, but the ascent of Sgurr Dubh Mor is a more exciting affair. Keep right to find a practicable line and on the final section follow scratch marks and cairns; the scrambling is mostly moderate with one or two moves that some may find hard.

The summit of Sgurr Dubh Mor is a narrow crest beyond which the ridge continues level for some distance before descending towards Coruisk to form a classic rock climb. For a taste of Dubh ridge climbing, scramble out along the level section of ridge on beautiful clean slabs of gabbro (add one hour to route time). For a different return route to Glen Brittle, descend northwards from Sgurr Dubh na Da Bheinn to the Bealach Coir' an Lochain and then choose a route from those listed on the opposite page.

Route 12: **THE SOUTH CUILLIN RIDGE**

OS MAP: 32 or OL8
Starting point: Glen Brittle campsite
(GR: 414205)
Route type: return mountain
scramble (or add-on to Route 11)
Distance: 9 miles (14km)
Ascent: 1,270m (4,150ft)
Time: 9 hours return by outward
route, or 4½ hours add-on to Route 11

	1	2	3	4	5
Grade				●	
Terrain					●
Navigation					●
Seriousness					●

Assessment: a magnificent stravaig along the easiest section of the Cuillin ridge, with the best views in the range.

Coruisk note: from Coruisk, Gars-bheinn's east ridge makes an interesting easy ascent. Reaching the foot of the ridge can be problematical owing to rocky ground above the shore but, higher up, the ridge narrows pleasantly and towards the summit passes some fine crags overlooking Coire a' Chruidh.

The southern end of the main Cuillin ridge, south of Sgurr Dubh na Da Bheinn, is the easiest lengthy section of ridge in the whole range and provides a wonderfully airy walk and easy scramble. The approach is as for Route 11, gaining the main ridge north of Caisteal a' Garbh-choire via Coir' a' Ghrunnda. From here the route southwards begins by following a path around the far side of the Caisteal to the Bealach a' Garbh-choire at the foot of the north ridge of Sgurr nan Eag (the traverse of the Caisteal is a rock climb).

If you keep to the crest, the ascent of the north ridge is more than a scramble on occasion, but all difficulties are avoidable on the right to give exhilarating scrambling of all grades on firm blocks of gabbro. A path further right makes the ascent barely more than a walk, and note also that both the Bealach a' Garbh-choire and Sgurr nan Eag can be reached easily by direct ascents from the lochan in Coir' a' Ghrunnda. The summit of Sgurr nan Eag is the third of three tors and lies at the far end of a 400-metre long, level summit ridge.

The route onwards to Sgurr a' Choire Bhig and Gars-bheinn, the two peaks at the end of the main Cuillin ridge, is a delightful high-level stroll, with wonderful views over Loch Coruisk on one side and Soay Sound on the other. The walk begins with a 150m (500ft) descent of Sgurr nan Eag's south-east shoulder. Scrambling can be sought at the cliff edge overlooking An Garbh-choire, where one deep chimney (after which the mountain is named: 'Notched Peak') can be crossed by a dramatic rock bridge.

The 100m (330ft) rise to Sgurr a' Choire Bhig begins gently, then narrows towards the summit. The crest of the ridge is barely more

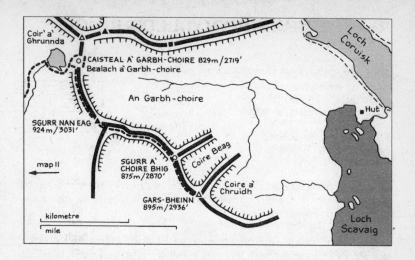

than an exposed walk, but a path below the crest on the right takes an even easier line. A short descent of 35m (120ft) follows, where it is necessary to put hand to rock on occasion, and then the main ridge ends with an extremely pleasant walk out to Gars-bheinn. Just before the short final rise to the summit, two stone shoots on the left are passed, the second of which contains a pinnacle that is accessible to those with sufficient nerve. Beyond the summit there are no more Cuillin, only the boundless sea.

The obvious return route on the map is down the southern flank of Gars-bheinn to the Coruisk–Glen Brittle coast path, but the steep scree slopes are horrendously tedious and difficult. It is much better to return along the ridge and descend by one of the routes noted for Route 11.

Route 13: **BLA BHEINN VIA COIRE UAIGNEICH**

OS MAP: 32 or OL8
Starting point: head of
Loch Slapin (GR: 561217)
Route type: circular mountain
walk
Distance: 6 miles (10km)
Ascent: 960m (3,150ft)
Time: 6 hours

	1	2	3	4	5
Grade			●		
Terrain			●		
Navigation				●	
Seriousness		●			

Assessment: a straightforward ascent through rocky surroundings to the summit of a Cuillin outlier that many consider to be the most attractive mountain on Skye.

'And over all broods the mighty mass of Blaaven, gleaming with rich purple, its clefts white with dazzling snow-wreaths, and wisps of cloud stealing around its secret top. It is a mountain among mountains, a king among them all, whose magic influence fills the heart. . .'

J.A. MACCULLOCH
(*The Misty Isle of Skye*, 1905)

When viewed across Loch Slapin from near Torrin, the shapely Cuillin outlier of Bla Bheinn presents one of the most compelling mountain sights in Britain. Several poets have been moved by it to put pen to paper, notably Alexander Smith, whose lengthy Victorian eulogy, beginning with the line 'O wonderful mountain of Blaavin', is worth keeping in mind as you toil up the stony summit slopes.

For ordinary mortals there are two easy routes to the summit in fine weather: via Coire Uaigneich and via the south ridge. Neither route need involve more than elementary handwork, although both give ample scope for scrambling of all grades. The Coire Uaigneich route is less scenic but is shorter and affords close-up views of the cliffs of the east ridge and the soaring rock tower of Clach Glas. It begins at the foot of the Allt na Dunaiche near the head of Loch Slapin on the A881 Broadford–Elgol road (parking beside a bridge 150 metres south). Take the path along the left bank (right side) of the river past some fine pools and waterfalls.

At the entrance to Choire a' Caise the path bears left across the Allt na Dunaiche and climbs steeply beneath the towering east face of Bla Bheinn into the bowl of Coire Uaigneich, a corrie that is unusually rich in Alpine flora owing to a small outcrop of Jurassic limestone. In the heart of the corrie the path turns sharp right to climb onto the skyline of the east ridge and meander up stony slopes to the summit. The path

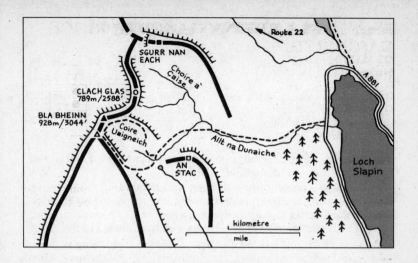

is indistinct in places but well cairned; scrambling routes can be sought and there are occasional glimpses of Clach Glas seen across the yawning gullies that drop from the east ridge into Choire a' Caise. The summit view of the main Cuillin ridge across the deep trench of Srath na Creitheach is superb.

A different descent route can be made by first crossing to the lower south top, which lies 200 metres away across a short dip whose negotiation requires some handwork. The obvious line up the south top from the dip between the two tops is along a ledge that gives an easy if slightly exposed scramble; an earthy gully a few metres down to the left provides an easier route (see also Route 14). From the south top, descend the steep, stony south-eastern slopes of the mountain to a small lochan at their foot; an indistinct path will be found in places. Cairns bear left in front of the lochan to mark a further stony descent into Coire Uaigneich; alternatively, continue to the dip a short distance beyond the lochan and descend grass slopes. Once into the corrie, rejoin the outward route.

Route 14: **BLA BHEINN VIA SOUTH RIDGE**

OS MAP: 32 or OL8
Starting point: Kilmarie
(GR: 545172)
Route type: circular mountain walk
Distance: 8 miles (13km)
Ascent: 1,100m (3,600ft)
Time: 6$\frac{1}{2}$ hours

	1	2	3	4	5
Grade			●		
Terrain		●			
Navigation	●				
Seriousness		●			

Assessment: an inviting ridge provides the most pleasant and scenic route to the summit of mighty Bla Bheinn.

Tigers' note: energetic rock climbers can combine the traverse of Bla Bheinn and Clach Glas with the traverse of the main Cuillin ridge to form the Greater Cuillin Traverse, a major test of mountaineering competence and stamina that involves nearly 4,300m (14,000ft) of ascent.

The Coire Uaigneich route up Bla Bheinn (Route 13) is the shorter and more popular of the two walkers' routes up the mountain, but the south ridge route described here is the more scenically and aesthetically pleasing. The ridge rises attractively in one clean sweep from the beautiful bay of Camasunary, giving superb views of the main Cuillin ridge across Srath na Creitheach and providing a surprisingly dry ascent even after rain. In many ways it provides a unique Cuillin ascent, much of it on grass, and it was famously described by an early guidebook as 'delightfully easy'; there is also plenty of opportunity for scrambling.

The route to the foot of the south ridge begins on the A881 Broadford–Elgol road 400 metres south of Kilmarie, from where a Land Rover track crosses the shallow bealach of Am Mam south of Bla Bheinn to Camasunary on Loch Scavaig. At Am Mam the sharp crest of the south ridge comes into view for the first time, rising evenly and invitingly from seashore to mountain top. Twenty metres before the hairpin bend on the descent to Camasunary (cairn), branch right on a path that cuts across the hillside and crosses the Abhainn nan Leac, which has some picturesque waterfalls, to the foot of the south ridge. Leave the path a couple of hundred metres beyond the river, at a large cairn on a boulder, and take the path that climbs the ridge.

The lower section of the ridge consists of steep grass slopes that lead to the craggy brow seen above. The path bypasses the crags on the right to reach the increasingly rocky upper ridge, whose solid gabbro is a pleasure to negotiate. Scrambling of all grades can be sought or avoided almost altogether by keeping to the path, which takes the line of least resistance. The ridge eventually merges with the south-eastern slopes of the mountain to culminate at the stony dome

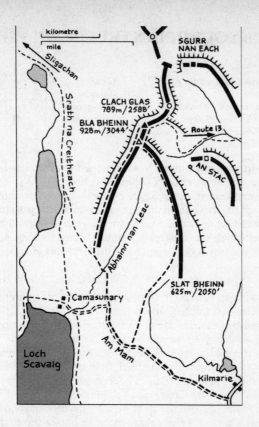

of the south top. The easiest route to the higher north top and summit 200 metres away descends a steep earth gully to just below the dip between the two tops. A more direct and interesting route involves an easy if slightly exposed scramble along a ledge on the left near the top of this gully (see also Route 13).

In fine weather a return via the lochan-studded plateau of Slat Bheinn makes a delightful contrast to the ascent route. From the south top, descend the south-eastern slopes of the mountain that rim Coire Uaigneich, as for Route 13. From the small lochan at the foot of the slopes a pleasant stroll across the flat, grassy plateau, with its many clear moorland lochans, leads back to Am Mam and the Land Rover track back to Kilmarie.

Route 15: **SGURR NA STRI**

OS MAP: 32 or OL8
Starting point: Sligachan
(GR: 486298)
Route type: return hill walk
Distance: 15 miles (24km)
Ascent: 580m (1,900ft)
Time: 8 hours

	1	2	3	4	5
Grade	●				
Terrain	●				
Navigation			●		
Seriousness		●			

Assessment: a long but easy walk to a perfectly sited miniature mountain at the heart of the Cuillin.

Pointless argument note: Sgurr na Stri's name (meaning Peak of Strife) is said to derive from an eighteenth-century boundary dispute between the MacLeods and MacKinnons, each of whom laid claim to the land on which the mountain stands. A compromise was agreed, but the dispute was soon forgotten as the land was of no use to either clan.

Sgurr na Stri is an extremely complex and rocky mountain that stands on the shores of Loch Coruisk and Loch Scavaig. Its ascent is characterised by stunning views and a long but magnificent approach walk, which makes the route a considerable undertaking.

Begin at the old bridge at Sligachan and take the excellent path that makes its way southwards along Glen Sligachan between the rounded Red Hills and the jagged Cuillin. The first feature of interest reached is the Clach na Craoibhe Chaoruinn (Stone of the Rowan Tree), which stands beside the path on the right a short distance beyond the Allt na Measarroch. After 3½ miles (6km) the path passes the deep trench of Harta Corrie, in whose mouth can be seen the curious Bloody Stone (see Route 2).

Keeping straight on along the main glen, the path forks at the foot of Am Fraoch-choire after a further ½ mile (1km). The right branch leads to Sgurr na Stri across the broad flats of upper Srath na Creitheach, a remote basin that has an air of spaciousness unequalled in the Cuillin. The conjunction of the flat floor of the strath and the steep western wall of Bla Bheinn behind gives the place the appearance and scale of an Alpine cirque. The path climbs to a large cairn on Druim Hain, from where the sparkling waters of Loch Coruisk and Loch Scavaig can be seen for the first time.

The main path appears to go straight on at the cairn, but this leads only to a viewpoint (worth the short detour). The true path goes left for a short distance to another large cairn, then forks. Keep left for Sgurr na Stri (the right branch descends to Coruisk: see Route 16). The path crosses the hillside below Sgurr Hain and after about 20 minutes

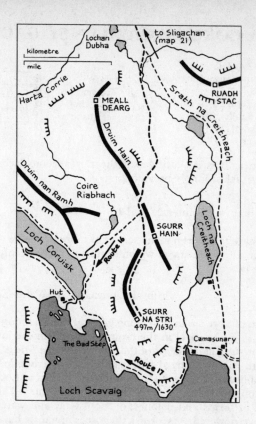

passes Captain Maryon's Cairn, which can be seen 100 metres below on the right. This 2m (7ft) stone pyramid was erected in memory of the captain after his body was found here in 1946. Five minutes further along, a stream drains a shallow grassy depression on the left that offers an easy way up to the complex series of rocky knolls that form the summit of Sgurr na Stri. The two most southerly knolls are the highest: one an eyrie above Camasunary, the other an eyrie above picturesque Loch Coruisk. The views in all directions are simply breathtaking.

The easiest return route is by the outward route, but energetic walkers should not miss the opportunity to descend to Coruisk and explore, and experienced Cuillin walkers may wish to consider the more serious return route to Sligachan over the Bealach na Glaic Moire (see Route 18b).

Route 16: **CORUISK VIA GLEN SLIGACHAN**

OS MAP: 32 or OL8
Starting point: Sligachan
(GR: 486298)
Route type: return hill walk
Distance: 15 miles (24km)
Ascent: 380m (1,250ft)
Time: 8 hours

	1	2	3	4	5
Grade	●				
Terrain	●				
Navigation	●				
Seriousness			●		

Assessment: a long but easy walk to the most spectacularly sited loch in the British Isles; simply breathtaking.

For sketch map, see Routes 21 and 15

'Though I have never seen many scenes of more extensive desolation, I have never witnessed any in which it pressed more deeply upon the eye and the heart.'

From the journal of Sir Walter Scott, 1814

If the Cuillin of Skye are the crowning glory of British mountains, then Loch Coruisk is the jewel in the crown. Cradled in the long narrow basin of Coir'-uisg at the heart of the remote eastern side of the range, studded with islands, fringed with sandy bays, surrounded by rocky peaks and only a stone's throw from the emerald seas of Loch Scavaig, it is justly famed for its rugged and picturesque scenery. There is such a profusion of forms and colours, on both land and water, that the senses are overpowered. At Coruisk the forces of nature have run wild.

Tourists came here to stand and stare long before the Cuillin were climbed. Sir Walter Scott came in 1814 while on a yachting tour of the west coast of Scotland. At his exhortation the painters William Danielson and J.M.W. Turner followed, and their paintings encouraged others. Early tourists came by boat across Loch Scavaig, and today it is still possible to take a boat from Elgol during the summer months, but to appreciate Coruisk to the full it must be explored on foot.

The easiest approach to Coruisk begins at Sligachan and takes the path along Glen Sligachan, as for Route 15. At the second fork on Druim Hain, when the left branch goes straight on to Sgurr na Stri, take the right branch down through Coire Riabhach to the lochside. NB: a short detour along the left branch affords magnificent views of Coruisk (see Route 15).

The best lochside view is obtained from the south-east shore (your arrival point), from where the prospect up the loch to the splintered

Cuillin skyline is exquisite. A short distance further away is the mouth of the loch, where the River Scavaig, renowned as one of the shortest rivers in the world, cascades into the sea at Loch Scavaig. The best viewpoint here is the knoll on the small peninsula that juts out into Loch Scavaig. In dry weather the River Scavaig can be crossed dryshod on stepping-stones at the mouth of Loch Coruisk. On the far side, hidden by a crag, is the hut belonging to the Junior Mountaineering Club of Scotland, with camping possible nearby. Return to Sligachan by the outward route or by the more serious crossing of the main Cuillin ridge at the Bealach na Glaic Moire (see Route 18b).

Walkers who have time to spend at Coruisk will find much to do. Paths along each side of the loch make a lochside circuit an attractive proposition and lead to Coir'-uisg, the rugged, complex amphitheatre of rock at the head of the loch. The renowned Bad Step on the Elgol coast path (see Route 17) is only a few minutes' walk away around Loch Scavaig. Ascents unique to Coruisk include Sgurr na Stri (see Route 15), Gars-bheinn via its east ridge (see Route 12), Druim nan Ramh, the Dubhs ridge (a rock climb) and Meall na Cuilce, a scramblers' viewpoint that offers stunning views of the area.

Route 17: **CORUISK FROM ELGOL**

OS MAP: 32 or OL8
Starting point: Elgol (GR: 520549)
Route type: difficult return coast walk
Distance: 12 miles (19km)
Ascent: enough
Time: 8 hours

	1	2	3	4	5
Grade				●	
Terrain				●	
Navigation		●			
Seriousness			●		

Assessment: one of the finest coast walks in the British Isles, leading to incomparable Coruisk. The route merits its Grade 4 rating for the Bad Step, which some may find Grade 5.

Conservation note: in 1968 the army built a bridge over the Abhainn Camas Fhionnairigh and proposed to dynamite the Bad Step in order to extend the Kilmarie–Camasunary track to Coruisk, but a public outcry prevented it. The bridge was soon destroyed by the elements. The Bad Step was left inviolate and long may it remain so.

The view of the Cuillin from the hilly village of Elgol is one of the most celebrated on Skye, and in terms of mountain scenery there is no finer coast walk in the British Isles than that around the shores of Loch Scavaig to Loch Coruisk at the heart of the Cuillin. The route is an adventurous one with a sting in the tail.

Begin in Elgol, just before the steepest part of the descent to the jetty. An access road heads uphill past a few houses and from its end a path continues across the grassy hillside below Bidein an Fhithich and Ben Cleat. At the foot of Glen Scaladal it descends to meadows before climbing around the slopes of Ben Leacach above vegetated cliffs at the water's edge. Easier slopes are reached at Rubha na h-Airighe Baine, and from then on the path keeps low down by the shore to the beautiful bay of Camasunary. Note that there is an easier route to Camasunary via a Land Rover track from Kilmarie (see Route 14).

Beyond Camasunary the route becomes immediately more exciting with the ford of the Abhainn Camas Fhionnairigh. At low tide the river can be forded at its confluence with a smaller stream just upriver from the remains of the old bridge; at high tide a much longer detour will be necessary. On the far side of the river the path follows the shoreline around the craggy slopes of Sgurr na Stri. At Rubha Ban, Gars-bheinn comes into view across Loch Scavaig and the scenery becomes increasingly wild. At the next headland (Rubha Buidhe) the path cuts through a defile on the right of a rocky knoll isolated from the main hillside. The top of the knoll provides a spectacular view of Loch Scavaig.

Coruisk looks close at hand now, but chaotic terrain on the western slopes of Sgurr na Stri makes the going painstakingly slow. At two

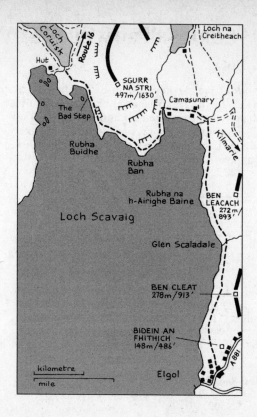

points boiler-plate slabs curve into the sea. The path rises over the top of the first but can find no way around the second – this is the infamous Bad Step, the negotiation of which is a moderate scramble with some exposure above deep water. Follow cairns down to the water's edge and clamber over huge blocks of rock that have fallen from the overhang above. Scramble round a corner and up a sloping crack, using finger-holds on the slab above the crack for safety. Half-way up the crack, go left along another horizontal fault onto easier ground (the temptation to continue straight on up the crack is what gets people into difficulties). Once past the Bad Step, it is only a few minutes' walk to the shores of Loch Coruisk.

Route 18: **CORUISK ROUTE MISCELLANY (1)**

OS MAP: 32 or OL8

Routes 18 and 19 are a compendium of five further routes linking Coruisk to Glen Brittle and Sligachan, from which to pick and mix. All involve handwork, rough terrain and navigational difficulty, and they should be considered serious propositions by walkers.

The following grid and map apply to all five routes. Distance/ascent/time shown apply one way only.

	1	2	3	4	5
Grade			●		
Terrain					●
Navigation					●
Seriousness					●

Route 18a
Starting point: Glen Brittle
campsite (GR: 414205)
Distance: 7 miles (11km)
Ascent: 300m+ (1,000ft+)
Time: 4+ hours

Route 18b
Starting point: Sligachan (GR: 486298)
Distance: 9¹/₂ miles (15km)
Ascent: 900m (2,950ft)
Time: 6¹/₂ hours

18a: The coast route to/from Glen Brittle

This is the only route from Glen Brittle to Coruisk that does not involve a crossing of the Cuillin, but it should not be taken lightly; it involves difficult route-finding on craggy slopes and one spot of slabby scrambling on the shores of Loch Scavaig that some people may find awkward. The route begins at Glen Brittle campsite and initially follows the Coir' a' Ghrunnda path. Avoid all left-branching lines up into Coir' a' Ghrunnda and keep straight on around the foot of the Cuillin to the Allt Coire nan Laogh. Beyond here the path takes to a long, gently rising grassy terrace before petering out on rocky ground. Cairns continue the line around Gars-bheinn almost 300m (1,000ft) above the sea, and it is important not to lose them.

Once you have followed the cairns up and around the gorge of the Allt an Fhraoich, avoid the temptation to descend too early. The cairned line stays high, making one more ascent before taking an obvious diagonal line down towards the shore beyond Eilean Reamhar.

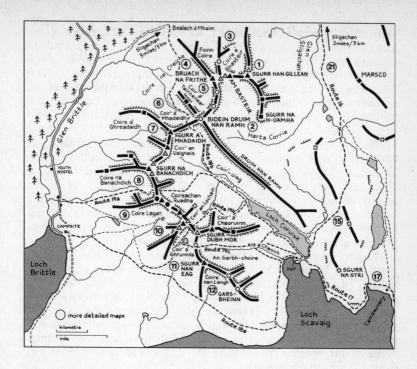

A path reappears and takes a line down that is even shallower than expected, eventually reaching the shore in the vicinity of the Allt a' Chaoich (the Mad Burn). Beyond the Mad Burn a section of boiler-plate slab by the shoreline involves a short, moderate scramble that may be awkward when wet and greasy. Once past here, Coruisk is only a few minutes' walk away.

In the direction Coruisk to Glen Brittle, the correct route is even harder to find.

18b: To/from Sligachan via the Bealach na Glaic Moire

This 760m (2,492ft) bealach between Bidein Druim nan Ramh and Sgurr a' Mhadaidh, at the head of Coir' a' Mhadaidh, is the lowest pass to Coruisk on the main Cuillin ridge. The route over the pass is marked on OL8 and is the shortest way between Sligachan and upper Coir'-uisg. In combination with Glen Sligachan (Route 16) it makes a magnificent round trip from Sligachan, but do not let the dotted line on OL8 mislead you into thinking there is a path – it is a steep, stony, awkward route and a much harder proposition than the low-level path along the glen.

45

In the direction Loch Coruisk to Sligachan, take either of the lochside paths to the head of the loch and Coir'-uisg; the south side of the loch gives slightly easier going. The level floor of Coir'-uisg is a combination of boulders and tussocky heather that makes heavy going, but a cairned path will be found on the left bank (right side) of the stream that bears right beneath the crags of Druim nan Ramh into the broad gully of the Glac Mhor (Big Defile). The bealach is at the head of this gully.

The gully rises past crags that guard the high corrie of Coir' an Uaigneis, and splits into two branches. The left (south) branch deposits you at the Sgurr a' Mhadaidh end of the bealach and is easier on ascent, with grass and rocks to ease the stony going. The right (north) branch deposits you at the Bidein Druim nan Ramh end of the bealach, and its loose stones are perhaps easier on descent. From the bealach it may be tempting to explore along the main ridge, but progress in either direction soon involves rock climbing.

To descend into Coir' a' Mhadaidh, first trend diagonally right from the Sgurr a' Mhadaidh end of the bealach down a broad grassy shelf beneath the crags of Bidein Druim nan Ramh. This traverse is necessary to bypass the corrie's craggy headwall and reach a stone shoot in the far right-hand corner of the corrie beneath the south-east ridge of Sgurr an Fheadain. Keep descending diagonally until you reach the head of the stone shoot (cairn; difficult to find in mist), then descend directly into the bowl of the corrie. The descent is stony, expletive-inducing but safe.

Lower down, pick up a path on the right bank of the developing stream and continue down beside a short gorge to reach a grassy area. Bear right here to follow a cairned line away from the stream beneath the cliffs of Sgurr an Fheadain; the route marked on OL8 continues down beside the stream but is longer and less straightforward than the right-branching route. At the foot of Sgurr an Fheadain the route joins a path that makes a rising traverse across the flanks of the north-west ridge of Bruach na Frithe to the Bealach a' Mhaim, and then it is downhill all the way beside the tumbling Allt Dearg Mor to Sligachan.

In the reverse direction, from Sligachan to Coruisk, the ascent of the stone shoot in Coir' a' Mhadaidh is purgatorial.

Route 19: **CORUISK ROUTE MISCELLANY (2)**

OS MAP: 32 or OL8

The following grid and Route 18 map apply to all routes. Distance/ascent/time shown apply one way only.

	1	2	3	4	5
Grade			●		
Terrain					●
Navigation					●
Seriousness					●

Route 19a
Starting point: Glen Brittle
Hut (or campsite) (GR: 411216)
Distance: 6 miles (10km)
Ascent: 850m (2,800ft)
Time: 5 hours

Route 19b
Starting point: Glen Brittle
campsite (GR: 414205)
Distance: 7 miles (11km)
Ascent: 850m (2,800ft)
Time: $5^{1}/_{2}$ hours

Route 19c
Starting point: Glen Brittle
campsite (GR: 414205)
Distance: 6 miles (10km)
Ascent: 800m (2,600ft)
Time: 5 hours

19a: To/from Glen Brittle via the Bealach Coire na Banachdich
This 851m (2,791ft) bealach between Sgurr na Banachdich and Sgurr Dearg connects Coire na Banachdich to Coireachan Ruadha, and provides technically the easiest way to Coruisk from Glen Brittle (coast route included). The route is marked on OL8, but this does not mean that there is a path or that it is an easy walk. See Route 8 for a detailed description of the Coire na Banachdich side.

To reach the bealach from Coir'-uisg on the Coruisk side, follow the stream that bears left around the leaning tower of Sgurr Coir' an Lochain into the large hollow of Coireachan Ruadha, one of the largest and most remote in the Cuillin. A cairned path will be found on the right bank (left side) of the stream. Higher up, keep well to the left of the stream to outflank waterfalls, then cut back right into the upper corrie and pick a route up steep slopes of boulders and scree at the back to reach the bealach. Note that this route also provides the most straightforward approach to the south ridge and rarely visited summit of Sgurr Coir' an Lochain, the last British peak to be climbed.

If descending to Glen Brittle from the bealach, the bouldery shelf that outflanks the craggy headwall of Coire na Banachdich (see Route 8) can be difficult to find, especially in mist. Descend a boulder ruckle until the crags on the left give way to bouldery slopes, then traverse left to pick up the line of cairns leading down into the corrie.

19b: To/from Glen Brittle via the Bealach Coir' an Lochain

This 855m (2,806ft) bealach between Sgurr Thearlaich and Sgurr Dubh na Da Bheinn connects Coir' a' Ghrunnda to Coir' an Lochain, two of the wildest corries in the Cuillin, and it is perhaps the most picturesque of all the passes over the main ridge. The Coir' a' Ghrunnda side of the bealach is a slope of boulders and scree. See Route 11 for a detailed description of the route from Glen Brittle to Coir' a' Ghrunnda.

On the Coruisk side, Coir' an Lochain is a high (580m/1,900ft), remote and magnificently untamed corrie that is approached from neighbouring Coir' a' Chaoruinn by a hidden terrace. Coir' a' Chaoruinn is a shallower corrie from which several streams descend over slabs to the head of Loch Coruisk. Starting at Coruisk, take the path along the south shore of the loch and climb left into Coir' a' Chaoruinn beside its first (southernmost) stream. The slabs cannot be avoided altogether, but the line of least resistance has little difficulty.

At about 400m (1,300ft) a large leaning slab on the right marks the start of a cairned terrace that makes a curious rising traverse around the slabby north-eastern slopes of Sgurr Dubh Mor, to emerge in Coir' an Lochain a short distance below the lochan. There are no more secret places in the whole Cuillin. The route to the Bealach Coir' an Lochain goes up grass and rocks at the back of the corrie to finish in a stone shoot.

19c: To/from Glen Brittle via the Bealach a' Garbh-choire

This 797m (2,614ft) bealach between Caisteal a' Garbh-choire and Sgurr nan Eag connects Coir' a' Ghrunnda to An Garbh-choire and leads almost directly to the mouth of Loch Coruisk. See Route 11 for a description of the Coir' a' Ghrunnda side.

Starting at Coruisk, there are several routes into An Garbh-choire. One follows the shore of Loch Scavaig as far as the Allt a' Chaoich (short moderate scramble required: see Route 18a) and then climbs between this stream and the next into the lower corrie. An easier route begins half-way along the south side of Loch Coruisk, climbs the shallow corrie on the south side of the Dubh slabs and then crosses the low ridge at its head into lower An Garbh-choire. Alternatively, from about 700 metres along the south side of the loch, cut back up a shallow depression onto the south-east ridge of Meall na Cuilce; this gives an easy and picturesque scramble over the top into the corrie.

Once into the corrie, follow the path up the left bank (right side) of the stream towards Caisteal a' Garbh-choire, the unmistakable rock fortress on the skyline. The path finds an easy route up the craggy steepening that separates the lower from the upper corrie and then loses itself among Herculean boulders. This upper section has a savage charm that may not be fully appreciated until you reach the skyline. The bealach is the gap on the main ridge left of the Caisteal.

Route 20: **GLAMAIG AND THE BEINN DEARGS**

OS MAP: 32 or OL8
STARTING POINT: Sligachan (GR: 487299)
ROUTE TYPE: difficult circular hill walk
DISTANCE: 7 miles (11km)
ASCENT: 1,230m (4,050ft)
TIME: 6¹/₂ hours

	1	2	3	4	5
Grade			●		
Terrain					●
Navigation			●		
Seriousness	●				

Assessment: a tough ascent leads to glorious views and ridge walking, in the shadow of the Cuillin, on the Red Hills.
Masochistic historical note: in 1899 the Gurkha soldier Havildar Harkabir Thapa reached the summit of Glamaig from the old bridge at Sligachan in 37 minutes, followed by a descent of 18 minutes. In bare feet! The current record, set in 1994, stands at 46.02 minutes.

Across the trench of Glen Sligachan the rounded granite peaks of the Red Hills line up incongruously against the bold gabbro peaks of the Black Cuillin. Ascents are tough (the geologist John MacCulloch named the hills 'Red' after their long fans of granite scree) but, once up, Red Hillwalking has much to recommend it. There are easy ridges to wander along and the views are superb. Glamaig is the epitome of Red Hills architecture, appearing from Sligachan as an enormous cone-shaped mountain that dominates the moor, and the view from the summit is exceptional even by Skye standards.

The best round in the Red Hills, traversing both Glamaig and its neighbours the Beinn Deargs, begins at Sligachan. The very steep, scree-riddled ascent from Sligachan to the summit of Glamaig requires more than the usual amount of motivation, but a *directissima* line to the summit does have a certain appeal. Grass rakes can be used to ease the going lower down, but these also require care, especially when wet. Aim right of the broken crags as viewed from Sligachan, and do not expect to stay upright all of the way.

From the summit, which is called Sgurr Mhairi (Mary's Peak), descend south-eastwards down steep scree runs to the Bealach na Sgairde. Care is required in mist as the natural trend of the summit ridge is out towards cliffs; the broken slope leading to the bealach is further right. From the bealach the steep stony ascent of over 300m (1,000ft) to the summit of Beinn Dearg Mhor looks monstrous, but secure good-sized rocks enable you to bound up in true Gurkha style (see note above) and the north ridge and summit are soon reached.

Beyond the summit of Beinn Dearg Mhor the going becomes

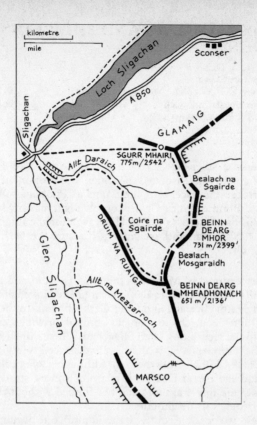

increasingly pleasant and interesting as the stony ridge leads on across the Bealach Mosgaraidh to Beinn Dearg Mheadhonach, which has a fine, narrow summit ridge a few hundred metres long. From here the descent back to the moor follows a cairned path down the summit boulderfield and along the level ridge of Druim na Ruaige, where there are welcome patches of turf to add some spring to the step.

From the end of Druim na Ruaige it is possible to descend either to the path along Glen Sligachan or, more interestingly, into Coire na Sgairde, where the Allt Daraich is as inviting as any Cuillin burn and where in summer dragonflies of many colours add to the picturesqueness of the scene. Lower down, a path follows the left bank of the Allt Daraich beside a wooded gorge that has some fine waterfalls and pools, and this path eventually meets the Glen Sligachan path near Sligachan.

Route 21: **MARSCO**

OS MAP: 32 or OL8
Starting point: Sligachan
(GR: 486298)
Route type: circular hill walk
Distance: 8^1/$_2$ miles (14km)
Ascent: 730m (2,400ft)
Time: 5^1/$_2$ hours

	1	2	3	4	5
Grade			●		
Terrain		●			
Navigation		●			
Seriousness	●				

Assessment: a steep but screeless ascent in the Red Hills, to the summit of an attractive isolated mountain and prominent viewpoint.
Charlie note: the ascent to the Mam a' Phobuill follows in the footsteps of Bonnie Prince Charlie on his flight across Skye in 1746. He used this pass to cross the Red Hills, avoiding the English redcoats stationed at Sligachan and exclaiming 'I'm sure the Devil would not find me now!'

The solitary sentinel of Marsco is the most isolated and attractive of the Red Hills. Separated from Beinn Dearg Mheadhonach to the north by a 280m (920ft) bealach and from Garbh-bheinn to the south by a 320m (1,050ft) bealach, its conical summit provides an attractive backdrop to the view along Glen Sligachan. When bathed in the warm glow of the evening sun, it may even distract attention from the shadowy Black Cuillin across the glen. Although geologically similar to Glamaig and the Beinn Deargs, it is a much more sturdy mountain that sports some fine crags and can be climbed without resort to the scree that bedevils its neighbours.

There are two possible routes to the summit, one beginning at Loch Ainort and one at Sligachan. The Loch Ainort approach ascends via Coire nam Bruadaran and Coire nan Laogh and is the shorter of the two, but it is mostly pathless and has no Cuillin views. The more aesthetic approach begins at Sligachan, from where the north-west ridge that forms the route of ascent can be seen in its entirety.

From Sligachan, follow the Coruisk path along Glen Sligachan (see Route 15) as far as the Allt na Measarroch, then leave it to follow another path up the near bank (left side) of that stream. The path continues as far as the bealach of the Mam a' Phobuill, where it becomes lost among sheep paths, but leave it before here to climb steep grass slopes to Marsco's north-west ridge and narrow summit. Higher up, the slope becomes very steep indeed, with some exposure, and you may well want to use your hands for balance.

The excellent all-round view from the summit encompasses the entire horseshoe Cuillin Ridge spread before you across the yawning depths of Harta Corrie, Loch Ainort and the isles of the Inner Sound,

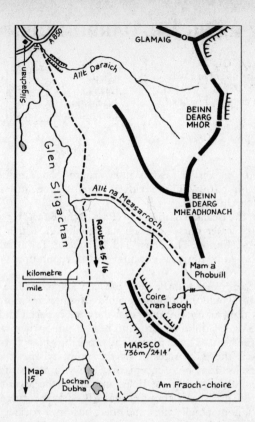

and rocky Bla Bheinn towering over the lump of Ruadh Stac. Note especially the distinctive colourings of Am Fraoch-choire beneath your feet, where the green grass slopes of Marsco meet the red rocks of Ruadh Stac.

For an alternative return route that provides a more gentle descent than the north-west ridge, continue over the top of Marsco and down the south-east ridge to a dip, then follow an old fence down around the eastern rim of Coire nan Laogh to the Mam a' Phobuill to regain the path along the Allt na Measarroch.

Note that it is also possible to extend the day by a descent southwards into Am Fraoch-choire and Glen Sligachan. The extremely rough direct descent from the dip into the corrie is not recommended, but the south-east ridge makes an interesting way down, with the waters of Am Fraoch-choire's beautifully clear stream beckoning below.

Route 22: BELIG AND GARBH-BHEINN

OS MAP: 32 or OL8
Starting point: head of Loch Slapin (GR: 563225)
Route type: circular mountain scramble
Distance: 6 miles (10km)
Ascent: 1,110m (3,650ft)
Time: 7 hours

	1	2	3	4	5
Grade				●	
Terrain					●
Navigation				●	
Seriousness		●			

Assessment: a varied, exploratory route that includes good scrambling on narrow basalt ridges, tough scree and impressive gabbro rock architecture.

Beast note: the Bealach nam Beiste (Pass of the Beast) is named after the legendary water horse of Loch na Sguabaidh, which was killed here by a MacKinnon. The beast had a penchant for attractive girls, and to be chased by him was good for a girl's reputation.

The trio of craggy peaks at the head of Loch Slapin make a rewarding scramble and would be climbed more often were it not for the proximity of the Cuillin; but note that the rock is basalt and therefore less adhesive than Cuillin gabbro, and best avoided when wet.

Begin at the head of Loch Slapin and cross the grassy flats above the road to reach the Allt Aigeann at the point where it disappears curiously into its stony bed (except after heavy rain). Continue to the foot of the south-east ridge of Belig and begin the ascent on short, sheep-cropped grass. At about 250m (800ft) the ridge steepens appreciably among small crags and then becomes rockier and more interesting. A prominent rock tower goes direct or can be avoided on the right, and then the crest of the ridge develops into a delightfully easy scramble, quite narrow and exposed in parts, but with no unavoidable problems.

The route onwards from the summit to Garbh-bheinn begins with a steep descent of the south-west ridge to the Bealach na Beiste. The upper part of the ridge would provide an interesting scramble were it not for a loose drystone wall on the crest that makes it necessary to resort to an indistinct path below on the right. Lower down, the ridge broadens and becomes uncomfortably stony, although scree can be sought to ease the descent. Similar awkward slopes rise from the bealach to Garbh-bheinn, but scrambling opportunities develop again near the summit.

The round continues down Garbh-bheinn's south-east ridge; this requires care at the top, where it is steep, broken and loose, but it develops into another pleasant scramble as it approaches the bealach below Sgurr nan Each. The scree slopes that descend left of the

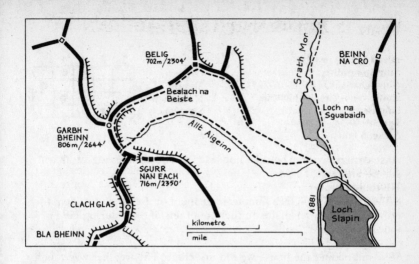

bealach are the descent route, but it is first worth exploring part of the way up Sgurr nan Each's west ridge. Half-way up, a level side ridge branches right towards the imposing gabbro rock tower of Clach Glas, and above this junction the ridge to Sgurr nan Each narrows suddenly across gabbro slabs to become a dead-end for walkers at another (impassable) rock tower. The side ridge to Clach Glas is also worth exploring as far as the bealach at the foot of Clach Glas, which looks spectacular from close up.

When you have finished exploring, descend the screes into the glen of the Allt Aigeinn, one of the most beautiful streams on Skye. Just before it turns to descend into the lower glen in a tiered waterfall, there is a series of pools and cascades that are breathtakingly beautiful, and all the way down the glen there are pools and waterfalls that make the descent to your starting point a constant delight.

Route 23: **BEINN NA CAILLICH**

OS MAP: 32 or OL8
Starting point:
Coire-chat-achan (GR: 619227)
Route type: circular hill walk
Distance: 5 miles (8km)
Ascent: 980m (3,200ft)
Time: 5 hours

	1	2	3	4	5
Grade			●		
Terrain					●
Navigation				●	
Seriousness		●			

Assessment: a steep boulder hop leads to a horseshoe ridge walk with superb and varied views.

Historical note:
SAMUEL JOHNSON's famous judgement on Beinn na Caillich, the only remark he ever made on the mountains of Skye during his 1773 tour of the island:

'The hill behind the house we did not climb. The weather was rough and the height and steepness discouraged us.'

Broadford's Beinn na Caillich is one of the most prominent hills on Skye, its bald grey dome towering over the moorland and capped by a huge cairn that is visible for miles around. The shortest and time-honoured ascent begins from near Coire-chat-achan at the end of the minor road that leaves the A850 just north-west of Broadford. It was from Coire-chat-achan that Thomas Pennant climbed Beinn na Caillich in 1772 to make the first recorded ascent of any mountain on Skye, and it was from here also that Johnson and Boswell did *not* ascend the mountain. The foreshortened view from Coire-chat-achan of the steep stony slopes of the Caillich is enough to give anyone pause for thought, and one may well feel the 'lethargy of indolence' that Boswell noted in his journal here. The ascent, however, is nowhere near as steep and formidable as it seems, for the rock has weathered into larger blocks than on the Red Hills further west and, once up, a fine horseshoe ridge walk leads onwards to Beinn Dearg Mhor and Beinn Dearg Bheag.

The best going on ascent will be found by aiming for the right-hand skyline. Once onto the bouldery hillside, any way up is as good as any other, so choose whichever boulder ruckle appeals and go for it. Boulder-hopping enables height to be gained fast; be patient with the convex slope and the unexpectedly grassy summit with its superb northern view will be reached without excessive effort. Beneath the huge summit cairn is said to lie a Norse princess, entombed here at her own wish so that she could forever face the land of her birth.

From the west end of the summit plateau (take care in mist) the

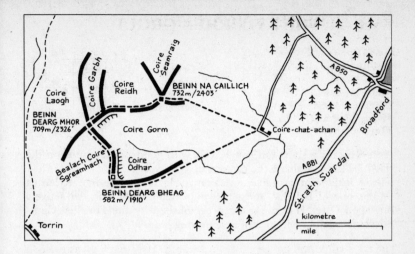

route continues around the tight horseshoe of Coire Gorm. The ridge descends pleasantly on grass and boulders to a bealach, then narrows attractively above steep corrie headwalls on each side to reach the stony summit of Beinn Dearg Mhor, with its magnificent view of Bla Bheinn. Steep, featureless scree slopes are then descended to the Bealach Coire Sgreamhach (take care in mist), and a short, rocky re-ascent gains the summit of Beinn Dearg Bheag, from where Rum can be seen across the Cuillin Sound.

To complete the horseshoe, descend the gentle ridge that curves down from Beinn Dearg Bheag's summit around Coire Odhar, picking up a path among the heather and boulders. Go straight off the end of the ridge down steep heathery slopes, cross the mouth of Coire Gorm and make a beeline back across the moor to your starting point. The going is rough, but the sweeping panorama of the glorious Inner Sound before you lures you homewards, with the island of Pabay set like a jewel in the sea.

Route 24: **THE KYLERHEA GROUP**

OS MAP: 33
Starting point: Bealach Udal
(GR: 756206)
Route type: return hill walk
Distance: 4 miles (6km)
Ascent: 760m (2,500ft)
Time: 4 hours

	1	2	3	4	5
Grade		●			
Terrain				●	
Navigation				●	
Seriousness	●				

Assessment: a short but rough walk with good coastal views on the two hills that dominate the eastern tip of Skye.

Lutra lutra note: unlike Kyleakin, peaceful bridge-free Kylerhea retains one of Britain's most thriving otter populations. An actively managed Otter Haven has been established by the Forestry Commission, together with a trail to a viewing hide.

Between the straits of Kyle Akin and Kyle Rhea stand the two commanding viewpoints of Sgurr na Coinnich and Beinn na Caillich. From Kylerhea ferry, their steep slopes rise directly from the sea to give an impression of great height, yet they are easily climbed from the 279m (915ft) Bealach Udal at the high point of the Kylerhea–Broadford road. On the opposite side of the bealach the lower Ben Aslak completes a trio of hills above Kylerhea that are characterised by rough terrain, numerous lochan-filled hollows and fine views.

The direct ascent of Sgurr na Coinnich from the Bealach Udal involves very rough going on tussocky grass and heather liberally strewn with boulders; easier going will be found further east, on the south ridge. Begin a few hundred metres east of the bealach, at the top of the steep descent to Kylerhea. Aim diagonally right, to the left of a prominent buttress, to gain the south ridge. The going gets easier as height is gained, and eventually becomes very pleasant on short turf. Look out for a beautiful lochan hidden in a hollow. Higher up, another lochan marks the start of the broad summit ridge, at the far end of which lies the highest point. From the summit there are tremendous views all around the compass: southwards is the Sleat peninsula; westwards over Broadford the Cuillin and the mountains of Strath crowd upon each other; northwards lies the Inner Sound, with Kyleakin at your feet; and eastwards are Kylerhea, Loch Alsh and the mainland peaks.

Beinn na Caillich is separated from Sgurr na Coinnich by the deep Bealach nam Mulachag, whose negotiation involves a 150m (500ft) descent and re-ascent that must be repeated in reverse on the return journey to the Bealach Udal. From Sgurr na Coinnich, Beinn na Caillich appears as a steep stony dome, but a route to the summit can

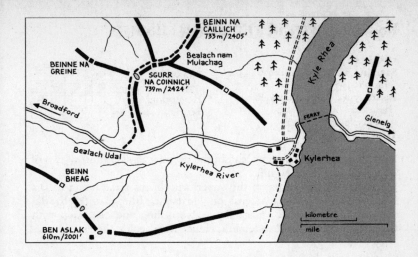

be picked out on grassy rakes to ease the going; the ascent is worthwhile for the unrivalled summit views of the kyles and Loch Alsh. The mountain's name (Mountain of the Old Woman) derives from Grainnhe (wife of Fionn, chief of the Fiennes), who is said to be buried at the summit.

Note: Ben Aslak on the far side of the Bealach Udal is a less imposing hill than its two neighbours, but its attractive and complex summit makes a good objective for a short tramp. From the bealach, climb heathery slopes towards the summit of Beinn Bheag, then cut left across the Kylerhea River onto the north-west ridge of Ben Aslak. Short turf and rock ease the ascent to the broad and knobbly summit ridge, which has good views, a top at each end and a fine lochan in the middle.

Route 25: **MACLEOD'S TABLES**

OS MAP: 23
Starting point: near Orbost
(GR: 256445)
Route type: circular hill walk
Distance: 7 miles (11km)
Ascent: 750m (2,450ft)
Time: 5½ hours

	1	2	3	4	5
Grade		●			
Terrain		●			
Navigation					●
Seriousness	●				

Assessment: steep ascents lead to the peculiar flat summits of two of Skye's most celebrated hills.

Legendary note: to prove the superiority of his banqueting hall, a MacLeod chief hosted a feast on Healabhal Bheag, with the flat summit as his table, a starry sky as his ceiling and clansmen with flaming torches as his candelabra. Hence MacLeod's Tables.

Healabhal Mhor and Healabhal Bheag are curious truncated hills that are more familiarly known as MacLeod's Tables. It is as though their summits have been lopped off by some supernatural force, and legend has it that this is precisely what happened, in order to provide a bed and table for St Columba when he was turned away from the door of a local clan chief (hence their Gaelic name, meaning Big and Little Holy Mountains). Geologists have a more prosaic explanation for the shape of the hills: it reflects the horizontal stratification of the basalt lavas of which they are composed.

Of the two Tables, Healabhal Mhor is the more often climbed, being closer to Dunvegan and having the larger summit plateau (hence its name, 'Big', although it is of lesser height), but Healabhal Bheag is the more interesting hill in all other respects. The best starting point for the round of both hills is somewhere between them on the Orbost road. From the roadside, head westwards across the moors of Glen Osdale, gain the broad east ridge of Healabhal Mhor and follow it to the summit. The ridge is enlivened by one or two rock bands and has fine views over Loch Dunvegan, but its most appealing attribute is its brevity.

The uniform steepness of the grassy upper slopes of Healabhal Mhor accentuates the flatness of the mossy summit plateau. The summit cairn, surprisingly large considering the lack of building material, lies at the far right-hand corner. The view is notable for its non-existence, for the edges of the table form a truncated horizon; on a hazy day you could almost be on a platform in the sky that has no visible earthly support.

To continue the round, descend to An Sgurran, cross Beinn na h-Uamha and climb steep grass slopes to the summit of Healabhal

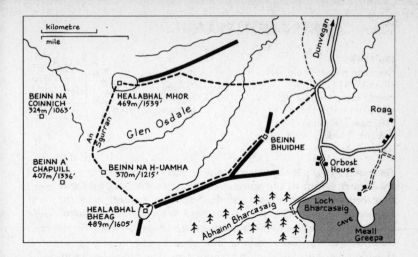

Bheag. The summit plateau is not as vast as Healabhal Mhor's, but it is equally table-like, and the view over Loch Bracadale is stunning, especially when evening light picks out the headlands and islands. The highest point on the plateau appears to be a grassy mound in the far south-west corner, from where the interesting south ridge falls away to the moor, giving opportunities for scrambling. Few, however, would wish to descend this way onto the featureless low hills of southern Duirinish.

To complete the round, descend Healabhal Bheag via its north-east ridge. This soon narrows onto the top of an impressive buttress, which in the evening casts a perfect pyramidal shadow onto the moor below. Circumnavigate the buttress on steep broken slopes to the left and continue down the ridge past one or two rises. Go over Beinn Bhuidhe or bypass it on the right to reach your starting point.

Route 26: **BEN TIANAVAIG**

OS MAP: 23
Starting point: Penifiler
(GR: 489417)
Route type: circular hill
and coast walk
Distance: 4$^1/_2$ miles (7km)
Ascent: 440m (1,450ft)
Time: 4 hours

	1	2	3	4	5
Grade		●			
Terrain	●				
Navigation		●			
Seriousness	●				

Assessment: a pleasant stroll along an interesting shoreline, followed by a short ascent to the summit of an isolated hilltop and viewpoint that forms its own peninsula on the Sound of Raasay.

Caves note: Ben Tianavaig's northern sea cliffs are holed by large caves, but there is no shoreline route to them. Beyond the skerries described in the text is a long stony beach, and then a nightmarish sheep path continues along a perilous grass shelf to a dead-end.

Ben Tianavaig is the high point of the peninsula to the immediate south of Portree and is a magnificent viewpoint for Raasay and the east coast of Skye. In appearance it has much in common with the hills of Trotternish to the north, with uniform, mostly unbroken slopes on the west (giving the hill an attractive pyramidal shape) and tiers of cliffs formed by landslips on the east. The upper slopes are composed of porous gravel, with large expanses of short turf that remains remarkably dry even in wet weather. The pleasant terrain and summit views make the ascent far more rewarding than you would expect from such a lowly hill.

The shortest route to the summit is from Camastianavaig on the B883 Braes road, but a more interesting circuit combines an ascent of Ben Tianavaig with an exploration of the coastline at its northern foot. The route begins at Penifiler, reached by a minor road that branches off the Braes road. From here, cross the neck of the Vriskaig Point peninsula to lonely Camas Ban, a broad, cliff-flanked strand of almost black sand (in spite of its Gaelic name, meaning White Bay). Ruins reflect the bay's former importance as a source of lignite.

From Camas Ban, follow a good path westwards over small shoreline crags to a larger, stony bay. At the end of this bay more crags force you up onto a broad grass shelf some 20m (65ft) above the sea, where a good sheep path provides excellent coast walking close to the cliff edge. Soon another bay is reached, enclosed by skerries that are a popular meeting place for a great variety of seabirds. It is worth descending to the bay to explore the rock pavement at the water's edge,

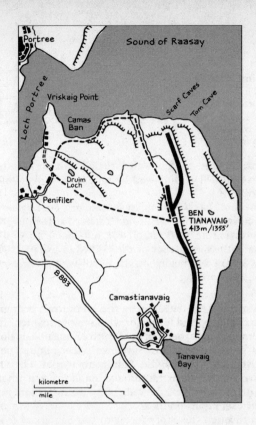

where rock buttresses project seaward like fingers. There are a few small caves.

Leave the coast at this point for the ascent of Ben Tianavaig. Two streams come down to the shoreline; climb the hillside between them, passing some ruined dwellings a short distance up. Continue directly to the summit; the going, as noted above, is excellent.

The summit is perched close to the edge of the broken cliffs of the east face and is one of the best viewpoints on the east coast of Skye, with an incomparable panorama of Raasay. In the basin below are a number of pinnacles similar to those at the Storr and Quiraing. To return to Penifiler, go straight down Ben Tianavaig's steep western slopes, negotiating one or two easy rock bands on the way. Plan your descent route at the summit, aiming left of a line of small cliffs and Druim Loch, because once you reach the flat moor, navigation is difficult.

Route 27: **THE STORR**

OS MAP: 23
Starting point: Storr Forest
(GR: 511531)
Route type: return hill walk
Distance: $3^1/_2$ miles (6km)
Ascent: 550m (1,800ft)
Time: 4+ hours

	1	2	3	4	5
Grade			●		
Terrain		●			
Navigation			●		
Seriousness			●		

Assessment: a visit to the weird rock pinnacles of the highest mountain in north Skye, followed by an ascent to its summit above disintegrating cliffs.

Climbing note: '*The Old Man may be climbable but we didn't make an attempt.*' Victorian climber Harold Raeburn's famous throwaway remark, expressing an understandable reluctance to rope up. Don Whillans made the first ascent of the Old Man in 1955; the route is graded Very Severe and begins on the north-west face near the right-hand end of the overhang.

It is at the Storr that the backbone of the Trotternish peninsula begins to erupt into the contorted forms for which it is renowned. The view of the Storr from the coast road north of Portree must be one of the most famous and photographed on Skye, with the summit cliffs of the mountain given scale by the Old Man at their foot. The Old Man is only one of a number of extraordinary pinnacles that ring the basin known as the Sanctuary, and the walk up to the Sanctuary is one of the most popular excursions on Skye.

The path through the Storr forest to the Sanctuary from the car park at the foot of the Storr is seriously boggy and is best avoided until it has been improved. Alternative paths climb each side of the forest; the easiest route up at the time of writing follows the fence on the north side. The array of pinnacles that guard the secluded interior of the Sanctuary give it the aura of a prehistoric site, and you will want to spend some time exploring here. The famous Old Man in particular is like a megalithic stone. It teeters 50m (165ft) above its plinth and is undercut all around; the rock is so flaky that it comes away in your fingers. Nearby is the improbable Needle, a fragile wedge of rock with two 'eyes' left by fallen blocks.

Behind the Sanctuary tower the 200m (650ft) rotten summit cliffs of the Storr, split into five buttresses by deep dark gullies. The route to the summit follows a path around the foot of the cliffs on the right (north) to gain the north-east corrie above the crags of Coire Scamadal. A line of cairns then points the way up to a V-shaped nick in the skyline, where a grassy gully breaches the cliffs (a short section of

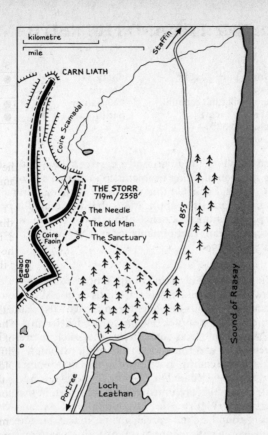

handwork is required here) to deposit you on the summit plateau not far from the trig. point.

The quickest route down is the route of ascent, but detours either northwards or southwards along the plateau can be used to add variety to the descent. The southward detour follows the plateau rim down to the Bealach Beag, then descends the left bank of the stream from here (another short section of handwork required) and crosses the moor to the south side of the Storr Forest. The northward detour follows the north ridge to the castellated rocky eminence of Carn Liath. The impressive northern cliffs of Carn Liath, hidden on approach, sport the cleanest climbing rock on the Storr, and beneath them is perhaps the most chaotic terrain in all Trotternish. The rarely visited summit is gained by an easy scramble on the south side.

Route 28: **THE FOX AND THE RED BANK**

OS MAP: 23
Starting point: Loch Cuithir
(GR: 476596)
Route type: circular hill scramble
Distance: 4 miles (6km)
Ascent: 520m (1,700ft)
Time: 3½ hours

	1	2	3	4	5
Grade				●	
Terrain			●		
Navigation		●			
Seriousness	●				

Assessment: a short circuit around a corrie skyline, but with enough scrambling and routefinding problems to give it an exploratory air.
Diatomite note: Loch Cuithir is floored with diatomite, a chalky earth with many industrial applications that was mined here until the 1960s. To permit mining, Loch Cuithir had to be drained, and the group of reedy lochans that remains today is the only remnant of what was once a large loch.

North of the Storr the hilly spine of the Trotternish peninsula gives an excellent end-to-end walk, characterised by gentle slopes on the west and an almost continuous line of cliffs on the east (see Route 31). The cliffs are incredibly complex owing to landslips, and the scenery created by these geological contortions is of such interest that three distinct areas are recommended for more detailed investigation (Routes 28–30). Heading northwards, the first points of interest reached are Sgurr a' Mhadaidh Ruaidh (Fox Peak) and Baca Ruadh (Red Bank). These hills are unusual for Trotternish in that they thrust out steep stubs of ridges to the east, enclosing Coir' an t-Seasgaich, and the short round of the corrie skyline makes an interesting and problematical route with plenty of opportunity for scrambling.

Access is by a rough but (normally) drivable road that runs westwards from the A855 Portree–Staffin road through the village of Lealt to picturesque Loch Cuithir at the foot of the massive eastern buttress of Sgurr a' Mhadaidh Ruaidh. The road was originally built to aid mining operations at the loch (see note above), but nature has now reclaimed the land and the area is very picturesque.

From the road end at Loch Cuithir, the route to the summit of Sgurr a' Mhadaidh Ruaidh begins by crossing grassy terrain to the foot of the ridge that forms the left-hand skyline. This ridge abuts rotten cliffs that offer no way up, but further left, on the far side of a shallow corrie, is another ridge whose broken slopes provide an easy, if sometimes earthy, scramble to the summit. The summit itself is perched airily at the cliff edge above Loch Cuithir, and offers grand views of the undulating Trotternish ridge and the vast flatlands of eastern Trotternish.

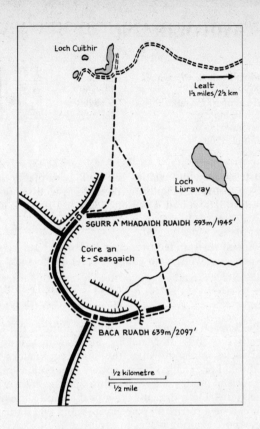

Baca Ruadh is easily reached by a pleasant stroll around the curving plateau rim above Coir' an t-Seasgaich, and then things become more exciting again. Descend eastwards, straight over the edge and down steep grass slopes, to reach the top of Baca Ruadh's eastern buttress. Crags bar a direct descent from here, but they are easily negotiated by a gully a short distance along on the right. Lower down, another hidden line of crags bars the way, but again these are easily outflanked a short distance along on the right, by a shelf that slants down right to easier ground.

To avoid all problems on descent, keep to the steep grass slopes that descend from the summit to the right of the buttress, then follow the foot of the buttress round. From here, cross the mouth of Coir' an t-Seasgaich, contour round the foot of Sgurr a' Mhadaidh Ruaidh and recross the moor to Loch Cuithir.

Route 29: **THE QUIRAING**

OS MAP: 23
Starting point: Bealach Ollasgairte
(GR: 440679)
Route type: circular hill walk
with optional scramble
Distance: 5¹/₂ miles (9km)
Ascent: 570m (1,850ft)
Time: 4+ hours

	1	2	3	4	5
Grade	●				
Terrain	●				
Navigation			●		
Seriousness	●				

Assessment: an easy but exciting hill walk, with plenty of enjoyable scrambling opportunities exploring the hidden recesses of one of the natural wonders of Scotland. The route's Grade 1 rating is for the main path only.

'You feel yourself surrounded by a crowd of mute figures, which seem as if they would fain whisper to you the secret of the ages.'

J. A. MACCULLOCH on the Quiraing
(*The Misty Isle of Skye*, 1905)

North of the Bealach Ollasgairte at the high point of the Uig–Staffin road, beneath the cliffs of Meall na Suiramach, stands a ghostly labyrinth of rocky spires known as the Quiraing. Visitors have come here to be thrilled or terrified for a century or more; in the heyday of Victorian tourism guides led tours through the narrow corridors between the spires. On a driech day, with the wind shrieking around the rocks, it can be a terrifying place indeed; but when the sun shines there are few more exciting places to explore.

Begin at the car park at the Bealach Ollasgairte and follow a fine path that is almost Alpine in character across the hillside into the Quiraing. Here the 36m (120ft) Needle stands opposite the castellated rocky eminence known as the Prison, whose entertaining summit ridge is the first formation that scramblers may wish to explore. To scramble even deeper into the heart of the Quiraing, leave the main path at a large cairn for a steep side path that climbs left of and behind the Needle, crosses the gully on its right and squeezes between two rock pillars to emerge into a fantastic pinnacled defile. At the head of this defile is the curious Table, a flat expanse of grass beneath the summit cliffs of Meall na Suiramach. After visiting the Table, retrace your steps to the main path or take a steep, rough short-cut to it down the gully right (north) of the Table (cairn at head of gully; keep right at a fork half-way down).

The path continues northwards along the foot of the main cliff face through complex country. Ignore all right-branching paths, which lead

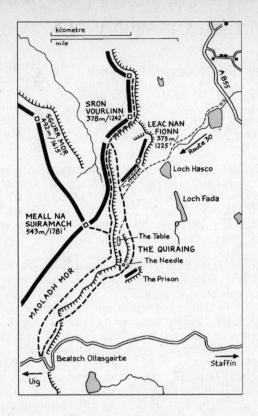

down to Loch Hasco (see Route 30), and cross the neck of land at the foot of the south-west ridge of Leac nan Fionn. The path eventually reaches the plateau north of Meall na Suiramach at a break in the cliffs (GR 449705).

Once onto the plateau, the short return trip northwards to the summit and north top of Sron Vourlinn is recommended for the spacious cliff-top walk and superb seaward view. Turning southwards, a return route can be made along the plateau rim, where grassy going makes for another fine cliff-top walk with magnificent views over the spires of the Quiraing to Staffin Bay and the offshore islands. Away from the cliff edge the plateau is mossy and yielding, and is best avoided except for the easily reached summit of Meall na Suiramach. Beyond the Quiraing the cliff edge becomes less well delineated and it is best to keep high, contouring along sheep paths, until a way can be made down the steep grass slopes of Maoladh Mor to the car park.

Route 30: **FINGAL'S PINNACLES**

OS MAP: 23
Starting point: near Flodigarry
(GR: 464710)
Route type: circular hill
walk with optional scramble
Distance: 3 miles (5km)
Ascent: 270m (900ft)
Time: 3+ hours

	1	2	3	4	5
Grade	●				
Terrain	●				
Navigation			●		
Seriousness	●				

Assessment: an easy hill walk on secret pinnacled hillsides, with plenty of enjoyable and exploratory scrambling opportunities.

Geological note: the landslips explored on this route are among the largest in Britain, extending 1¹/₂ miles (2km) to the coast. They were caused by the collapse of great cliffs on the eastern edge of the lava cap that covered Trotternish sixty million years ago.

To the north and east of the Quiraing, especially around the flanks of Leac nan Fionn (Fingal's Tombstone), landslips have created an astonishingly contorted terrain, full of knolls, crags, pinnacles and hidden lochans. To explore the area, begin on the A855 coast road just south of Flodigarry. Take the cart track to Loch Langaig, and then the path that continues from there to Loch Hasco beneath the cliffs of Leac nan Fionn; note the rock tooth that projects from the hillside up on the right.

Beyond Loch Hasco the path climbs diagonally across the hillside beneath the crags of the complex south-west ridge. Note the rock needle high up on the crest of the ridge. Breaks in the crags enable short-cuts to be taken up to the ridge, but it is more interesting to continue to the neck of land where the foot of the ridge abuts against the cliffs of Meall na Suiramach, then double back and climb the ridge to the summit. The ridge is beset with scrambling challenges, but gentle grass slopes to the left enable all obstacles to be easily bypassed. The first obstacle is a rock tower that provides a short sharp scramble to the clump of grass that crowns its top. Above here grass rakes rise between crags, right of which is the rock needle that was seen from below; the needle goes direct, providing an easy scramble to its airy top.

Beyond the needle, at the cliff edge above the east face, is the level grassy summit of Leac nan Fionn. The cliffs are split into four buttresses of approximately equal height. The rightmost (south) buttress is separated from the rest by a shallow notch whose negotiation involves a moderate, exposed scramble.

A descent northwards enables a circular route to be made via one of the unsung wonders of Trotternish: Pinnacle Basin. Make for the saddle that separates Leac nan Fionn from Sron Vourlinn; the direct

The classic Cuillin view: Sgurr nan Gillean (left), Am Basteir (centre), and Sgurr a' Bhasteir (right), viewed across the River Sligachan (*Route 1*)

Am Basteir, Sgurr nan Gillean and Sgurr a' Fhionn Choire from Bruach na Frithe (*Route 4*)

The Great Stone Shoot drops from the bealach between Sgurr Thearlaich and Sgurr Alasdair, with Sgurr Mhic Choinnich further left snd Sgurr Sgumain further right *(Route 10)*

Gars-bheinn from Sgurr a' Choire Bhig *(Route 12)*

Bla Bheinn from Torrin *(Route 13)*

Loch Coruisk from Sgurr na Stri *(Route 19)*

Glamaig and Beinn Dearg Mhor from Sligachan *(Route20)*

Snow-dusted Beinn na Caillich (centre)
from Beinn Dearg Mheadhonach *(Route 23)*

Ben Tianavaig, with the Storr behind; telephoto from Glamaig *(Route 26)*

The Old Man and other pinnacles of The Storr *(Route 27)*

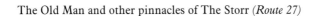

A wintry day on Stac Suisnish, with Bla Bheinn behind *(Route 32)*

The coastline from Gob na h-Oa to Rubha nan Clach, viewed from Oronsay *(Route 37)*

An eerie day at Moonen Bay, with wispy cloud on Ramasig Cliff *(Route 40)*

The wing-shaped Braes peninsula; telephoto from Glamaig *(Route 43)*

Dun Caan from Loch na Mna cliffs *(Route 48)*

The north end path above Loch Arnish, looking south along the spine
of Raasay to Dun Caan (centre left) *(Route 50)*

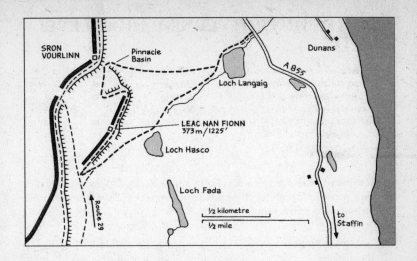

descent is barred by cliffs, but these are easily outflanked on the left (west). Once onto the saddle, aim for the lochan and the wall just beyond, then descend over the lip of the saddle into the secret hollow of Pinnacle Basin. Here, pinnacles rise from the hillside like prehistoric standing stones, each with an individual character that gains from its group setting; the most impressive pinnacle is reminiscent of the Old Man of Storr. There is plenty of climbing and scrambling to be done hereabouts.

On leaving the basin, aim diagonally right down the steep hillside to rejoin the approach path above Loch Langaig. On the way you should pass the rock tooth seen during the approach walk, and this provides an easy scramble to round off an entertaining route.

Route 31: **THE TROTTERNISH HIGH-LEVEL ROUTE**

OS MAP: 23
Starting point: Portree (end point Duntulm) (GR: 481436 (end point 411741))
Route type: one-way backpack
Distance: 26 miles (42km)
Ascent: 2,410m (7,900ft)
Time: 2 days

	1	2	3	4	5
Grade		●			
Terrain		●			
Navigation			●		
Seriousness		●			

Assessment: the finest backpacking route in the Hebrides, a grand skyline promenade along the undulating spine of Skye's largest and most northerly peninsula.

'Then onwards, ever northwards, down into the valleys and up again to the hill-tops... It was a walk along the top of the world, with glorious vistas of seas, islands and mountains.'

BEN HUMBLE
(*Tramping in Skye*, 1933)

From Portree to the north coast of Skye the backbone of the Trotternish peninsula forms a high escarpment, with gentle slopes on the west and a more savage line of cliffs on the east. The walk along the crest of the escarpment, known as the Trotternish High-Level Route, is one of the finest end-to-end expeditions in Scotland. The ridge reaches the 600m (2,000ft) contour at five points and crosses several other tops over 500m (1,650ft) high. Short turf makes for excellent going as the ridge undulates from top to top, with magnificent coastal views all around and the 'tangle o' the isles' to lighten your step.

The route leaves the roadside at the bridge over the River Chracaig about 1$^{1}/_{2}$ miles (2km) north of Portree. It begins unenterprisingly, with a boggy moorland stomp over the minor tops of Pein a' Chleibh and A' Chorra-bheinn to Ben Dearg, where the line of eastern cliffs that will be with you for the remainder of the trip first appears. The band of summit crags that bars the direct descent from Ben Dearg is outflanked by a long dog-leg to the west. Two passes (Bealach Mor and Bealach Beag) follow as the ridge undulates northwards and climbs steeply to the summit of the Storr (Route 27). To avoid the initial bogtrot (and Ben Dearg's crags), join the ridge beyond A' Chorra-bheinn or at the Bealach Mor.

On the far side of the Storr a steep descent and re-ascent across the Bealach a' Chuirn gains the summit of Hartaval, the second highest peak in Trotternish, and then comes a more gentle section culminating

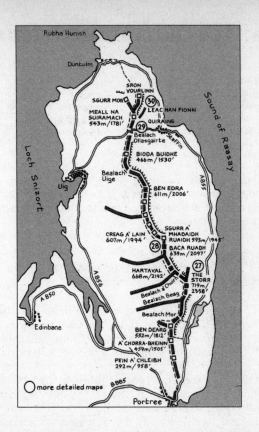

in Baca Ruadh and Sgurr a' Mhadaidh Ruaidh (Route 28). Continuing northwards, the ridge undulates over a succession of tops to Beinn Edra, the most northerly 600m (2,000ft) hill on Skye, before losing height at the Bealach Uige. A steep climb over the summit of Bioda Buidhe then deposits you at the Bealach Ollasgairte on the Uig–Staffin road; the descent to the bealach passes the craggy lump of Cleat, which is separated from the main ridge by landslips and towers over Loch Cleat.

North of the Bealach Ollasgairte the route reverses Route 29 to cross Meall nam Suiramach above the Quiraing and reach a fork in the ridge. On the left fork lies Sgurr Mor, whose yielding moss makes tough going. The better route is the right fork, where a spacious walk leads out along the narrow summit ridge of Sron Vourlinn above Leac nan Fionn (Route 30). Continue past the summit to the north top and descend across the moor to the A855 coast road. Duntulm, a few miles away on the north coast, makes a fitting end-point to the route.

73

Route 32: **SUISNISH AND BORERAIG**

OS MAP: 32 or OL8
Starting point: Loch Cill Chriosd (GR: 615205)
Route type: circular moor and coast walk
Distance: 10 miles (16km)
Ascent: 420m (1,400ft)
Time: 5+ hours

	1	2	3	4	5
Grade	●				
Terrain	●				
Navigation		●			
Seriousness	●				

Assessment: ancient moorland paths link to form an exploratory circuit visiting limestone scenery, sea cliffs, stacks and caves, old marble quarries, deserted villages, duns, Druidical sites and many other features of interest.

Goblin note: take care on this route not to be overtaken by darkness, for Strath Suardal is haunted by the malevolent goblin Ludag who, according to tradition, hops about on his one leg dealing 'heavy blows on the cheeks of benighted travellers'!

No part of Skye is more fun to explore than the stub of land that juts seawards between Loch Slapin and Loch Eishort in the south of the island. The best circuit around it begins in Strath Suardal on the A881 Broadford–Elgol road. From the corner of Loch Cill Chriosd, take the cart track that marks the start of an ancient, convoluted, indistinct path (marked on OL8) that passes through the ruined village of Kilchrist, a limestone oasis on the moor. Beyond Kilchrist the line of the path follows the shallow valley of the Allt an Inbhire to the head of the Allt nan Leac (see Route 33), then it crosses open moor, left of the prominent grassy knoll formerly crowned by Dun Kearstach, to the ruined village of Suisnish. In the vicinity of the dun it is better to leave the path and descend to join the Land Rover track from Camas Malag, then turn left into Suisnish. During the nineteenth-century Highland Clearances hundreds of people were brutally evicted from here.

The Land Rover track continues through Suisnish but misses an exciting stretch of coastline that is worth a diversion. Cut down the fields below the village to Stac Suisnish, whose two 5m (16ft) high tops provide good sport for boulderers, then continue along a rock pavement at the foot of overhanging 30m (100ft) sea cliffs around the point of Rubha Suisnish and past Calaman Cave. The walk along the pavement, although occasionally greasy, is a thrilling shoreline trip that can be undertaken AT LOW TIDE ONLY, with no escape for the next ½ mile (1km), until the point has been rounded.

From the end of the Land Rover track in Suisnish, continue straight on across a field to pick up the excellent old path to verdant Boreraig,

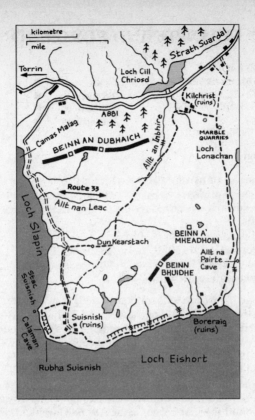

another ruined village where streams meander down to a lovely bay across green meadows. Using OL8 as a guide, seek out the dun, the site of the Druidical temple and the solitary standing stone.

To find the path out of the village, begin at the standing stone and head up to the right of some ruins. The path climbs steadily above the gorge of the Allt na Pairte, passing a large tree-filled hollow that is the entrance to Allt na Pairte Cave. Towards Loch Lonachan the path becomes quite boggy, but then it improves again as limestone country is reached once more on the descent towards Strath Suardal. The hillside at this point is dotted with spoil heaps from old marble quarries, whose marble is said to have been used in the building of the Palace of Versailles. Once the first spoil heap is encountered, cut down to Kilchrist to rejoin the outward route.

Route 33: **LIMESTONE CAVES OF STRATH**

OS MAP: 32 or OL8
Starting point: Camas Malag
(GR: 583193)
Route type: return coast and
glen walk
Distance: 4 miles (6km)
Ascent: n/a
Time: 3+ hours

	1	2	3	4	5
Grade	●				
Terrain	●				
Navigation	●				
Seriousness	●				

Assessment: an unusual and entertaining off-day excursion to the limestone centre of Skye. **N.B.** only expert cavers should enter the dangerously constricted cave interiors.
Cave lengths:
1 Camas Malag Cave 250m (830ft)
2 Uamh Sgeinne 105m (305ft)
3 Beinn an Dubhaich Cave 175m (570ft)
4 Uamh Cinn Ghlinn 365m (1,200ft)

The limestone landscapes of Strath are a delight to explore. Much fun can be had searching for cave entrances, and in the vicinity of the glen of the Allt nan Leac there are four 'through' caves whose underground meanderings can be followed on the surface from one entrance to the other.

The route to the Allt nan Leac begins at the bay of Camas Malag, reached by a minor road that leaves the A881 just east of Torrin. Beyond the bay the road continues as a rough Land Rover track to Suisnish. Around the first corner is the Allt na Garbhlain, which sinks into a large hole on the right to form the upper entrance of Camas Malag Cave, the first of the 'through' caves. Lower down the hillside the stream reappears at other entrances before exiting from the system at a fissure in a shoreline cliff, which can be reached by a short scramble.

Continuing along the track to Suisnish, the next stream reached is the Allt nan Leac itself. Aim for the small waterfall that can be seen less than 100 metres upstream; to its left a small stream emerges from the hillside, disappears underground and reappears again. The upper resurgence (a low arch of rock) is the lower entrance to the Uamh Sgeinne (Cave of the Knives). The upper entrance burrow lies less than 100 metres further upstream, but finding it will test your powers of observation – it is hidden among limestone outcrops, about ten metres up the hillside from a point where trees stand on each side of the Allt nan Leac just below a small waterfall and pool.

Above the Uamh Sgeinne the glen levels off. Fifty metres beyond the point where a fence crosses to the near bank (left side), there is a

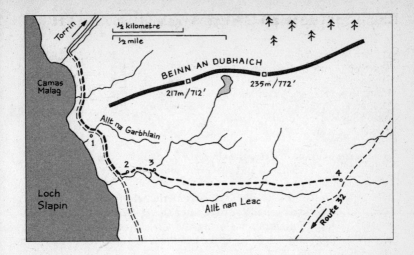

resurgence a few metres to the left. This is the rising for Beinn an Dubhaich Cave, whose main entrance, a 3m (10ft) deep tree-covered hole, can be found about thirty metres diagonally uphill further right. Further right still is the upper entrance, where the stream sinks underground.

Beyond the level section of glen containing Beinn an Dubhaich Cave, a slight rise leads to another long flat section, and then the glen narrows and climbs to yet another short flat section where an old wall is crossed. One hundred metres beyond the wall, a tree marks the spot where the young Allt nan Leac emerges from a hole at the foot of a line of crags. This is the lower entrance of the Uamh Cinn Ghlinn, the longest and finest cave on Skye. The two upper entrances can be found by following the dry valley up onto the moor. Return to Camas Malag by the outward route.

Route 34: **RUBH' AN DUNAIN**

OS MAP: 32 or OL8
Starting point: Glen Brittle
campsite (GR: 414205)
Route type: circular coast walk
Distance: 7½ miles (12km)
Ascent: n/a
Time: 4½ hours

	1	2	3	4	5
Grade	●				
Terrain	●				
Navigation	●				
Seriousness	●				

Assessment: a stroll along the shores of Loch Brittle, in the shadow of the Cuillin, to a headland and viewpoint where there are many features of historical interest.

Historical note: the headland was formerly held by the MacAskills, who turned to fishing and farming after the last clan battle on Skye in 1601. Despite emigration during the Clearances, there were still twenty or more families living at the headland in 1883. Today nothing remains but ruins.

From Glen Brittle the low-lying headland of Rubh' an Dunain does not appear as inviting as the majestic Cuillin that tower above it, yet the route to the point provides a pleasant coast walk with fine views of Rum, Canna and the southern Cuillin corries, with much to see at the headland itself.

From Glen Brittle campsite a farm track runs along the coast as far as the second stream beyond the Allt Coire Lagan (bridge downstream), then a path continues. When the path forks at the stream just before Creag Mhor, whose 15m (50ft) basalt crags provide sport for rock climbers when the Cuillin are in cloud, keep right to reach the northern end of the Slochd Dubh (Black Pit), a fault line that cuts right across the headland. Easy ground then continues around the north and west slopes of Carn Mor to Loch na h-Airde, where exploration of the headland begins.

In front of the wall beside the loch is a well-preserved chambered cairn, with a 3m (10ft) long, 1m (3ft) high passageway leading into the central chamber, now roofless. When the chamber was excavated in 1931 and 1932 the remains of six adults and pieces of pottery were unearthed, dating its use to the Beaker and Neolithic periods. From here, walk out to the point of the headland, where a cairn caps small sea cliffs and there are fine views of Rum, only 8 miles (13km) away across the sea. Next, continue around the headland to the mouth of Loch na h-Airde to view the channel that was built long ago to link the loch with the sea and enable it to be used as an anchorage for galleys. The dun after which the headland is named crowns a knoll on the far side of the channel, its landward wall still 4m (13ft) high, its seaward side guarded by cliffs.

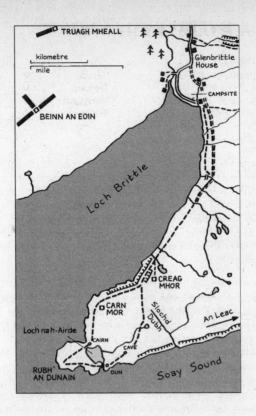

On the hillside east of the loch is a shallow cave, which revealed Beaker pottery and an Iron Age forge during excavation in 1932. By following the stream left of the cave up towards a small lochan, the ruins of Rhundunan House (the old MacAskill home) can be seen. To return to Glen Brittle campsite from here, recross the headland via the Slochd Dubh and rejoin the coast path. To vary the return route from the Allt Coire Lagan if the ground is dry, drop down to a lower path that passes some interesting rocky inlets.

Adventurous walkers can extend the walk by following cliff-top sheep paths along the southern coastline from the Rubha to the Allt na Meacnaish waterfall and An Leac (The Flagstone), the only landing place on the Soay Sound and the old ferry point for crossings between Skye and Soay.

Route 35: **BRITTLE TO EYNORT**

OS MAP: 32
Starting point: foot of
Glen Brittle (GR: 409210)
Route type: circular cliff-top
coast and moor walk
Distance: 7½ miles (12km)
Ascent: 490m (1,600ft)
Time: 6 hours

	1	2	3	4	5
Grade				●	
Terrain				●	
Navigation					●
Seriousness			●		

Assessment: a rough and serious coast walk to a remarkable sea stack. The route involves no scrambling but is graded 4 to reflect its challenging nature.

Petticoat note: When Sarah Murray sailed into Loch Eynort in 1802, the Stac an Tuill seemed to her 'like a lady dressed in a monstrous sized hoop and petticoat, having a very large hole quite through the middle of the hoop'.

North of Loch Brittle are to be found the first great sea cliffs of the west coast of Skye and one of the island's most fantastic sea stacks: Stac an Tuill (Stack of the Hole). The walk, however, is a serious one, as the convex, crumbling cliff edge is one of the most dangerous on the coast and the return across the Minginish moors is rough.

The route begins at the footbridge over the River Brittle near Glen Brittle campsite. Follow the rocky western shoreline of Loch Brittle below fields and fences and then continue along an obvious grass shelf above the shore. Keep to this shelf until it crosses a stream that cascades from the moor above and begins to peter out on increasingly steep slopes, then make a steep, rising traverse onto the moor, aiming for the top of an open gully seen ahead. Once onto the cliff top, continue out towards the headland at the mouth of Loch Brittle, passing two fine lochans.

The coastline now turns north-westwards and the cliff edge becomes more undulating and complex. It is best to keep to sheep paths well back from the edge, and aim for the rocky high point of Dunan Thearna Sgurr ahead. Beyond Dunan Thearna Sgurr the cliffs become more awesome and the direct route onward is immediately barred by the deep gorge of the Allt Mor and its 15m (50ft) waterfall; this is negotiated by contouring into the glen above the waterfall and crossing the stream there. Beyond the gorge the cliff top is turfed with short grass and gives excellent walking, but again stay well clear of the cliff edge, where in places crumbling earth perilously overhangs the abyss.

The cliff top reaches its highest point at Sgurr nam Boc, but do not attempt to view the plunging 217m (712ft) cliff face until you get to

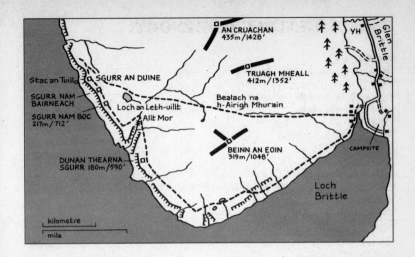

Sgurr nan Bairneach, the next headland beyond. From here the intricate, perfectly sculpted Stac an Tuill can also be seen for the first time. The complete structure resembles a gothic cathedral, complete with spire and vaulted window (the 'hole'). For a closer view of the stack, continue to Sgurr an Duine (the headland above it), and descend to the next headland beyond, from where you can see it more clearly.

Beyond here the sea cliffs diminish in size and interest towards Loch Eynort. To return to Glen Brittle, leave the coast, aim left of the marshy shores of Loch an Leth-uillt and cross the Bealach na h-Airigh Mhurain. The tramp across the moor is very rough; it seems a long time before the long flat bealach is reached and the Cuillin burst into view to beckon you homewards.

Route 36: **EYNORT TO TALISKER**

OS MAP: 32
Starting point: foot of Glen Eynort (GR: 379264)
Route type: circular cliff-top coast and moor walk
Distance: 13$^{1}/_{2}$ miles (21 km)
Ascent: 440m (1,450ft)
Time: 10 hours

	1	2	3	4	5
Grade					●
Terrain		●			
Navigation					●
Seriousness				●	

Assessment: a thrilling coast walk: exposed, serious, lonely and full of stirring situations. The route involves no scrambling but is graded 5 to reflect its challenging nature.

Rock note: the rarely viewed south-west face of fortress-like Preshal Beg is noteworthy for its fluted basalt pipes, in comparison with which the similar formations at the Giant's Causeway in Antrim seem but an inferior imitation.

Peaceful Glen Eynort is the ironic starting point for the most spectacular of the Minginish coast walks, northwards along the cliff top to Talisker Bay. Begin at the road end in Eynort village and continue along an unsurfaced road and path to the small peninsula of Faolainn. Beyond Faolainn a good sheep path continues along a grassy shelf above small waterside crags and then the route takes to the beach. At the point beyond Faolainn the hillside above the shore (Biod na Fionaich) steepens, but rock pavement at the shoreline continues to provide a curiously exciting promenade, clinging to the edge of the land.

At the point beyond Biod na Fionaich, sea cliffs bar the route and it is necessary to climb steep grass slopes to higher ground; some of the ascent is very steep indeed and requires care. Keeping well away from the crumbling cliff edge, you are forced upwards to a height of 90m (300ft) at the headland above the sea caves marked on the map. Continue across the hanging valley of Tusdale and keep high, right of Sgurr Mor (the headland at the mouth of Loch Eynort) to regain the cliff top at Glen Caladale.

Between Glen Caladale and the next headland of Sgurr Beag, a fine wide bay backed by a line of 90m (300ft) cliffs gives a taste of the excitement to come, for the route now develops into a wonderful cliff-top stravaig on short grass and good sheep paths. As you progress, the coastal architecture becomes increasingly impressive. Beyond Sgurr Beag the great grass-topped stump of Stac a' Mheadais is passed en route to the airy viewpoint of Sgurr Buidhe. The route then undulates for 2 miles (3km) above a line of unbreached cliffs, surmounting the huge cliff face of Sgurr nam Fiadh and passing crag-girt Preshal Beg

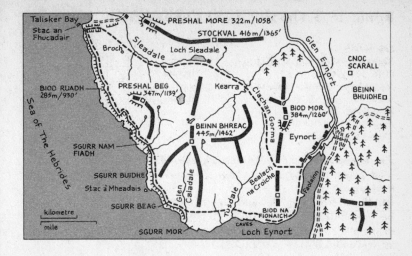

on its way to the summit of Biod Ruadh. This, the highest point on the walk, is marked simply by an airy tuft of grass teetering on the edge of a sensational 285m (930ft) drop.

Beyond Biod Ruadh the cliffs diminish in height towards Talisker Bay. Descend along the cliff edge, detouring around one or two rock bands, to reach the headland above Stac an Fhucadair at Talisker Point (see Route 37). Turn right here and head eastwards, making a rising traverse into Sleadale beneath the impressive prow of Preshal More. From Sleadale the return route to Eynort takes a long but surprisingly level route through the hills. Follow the Sleadale Burn up to remote Loch Sleadale, then descend across the broad basin of Kearra and continue through the curious grassy corridor of Clachan Gorma. When the river begins to descend into Tusdale, contour left onto the Bealach na Croiche and descend to Eynort.

Route 37: **TALISKER TO FISKAVAIG**

OS MAP: 32
Starting point: Talisker Bay
(GR: 326306)
Route type: circular cliff-top
coast walk
Distance: 7$\frac{1}{2}$ miles (12km)
Ascent: 290m (950ft)
Time: 5 hours

	1	2	3	4	5
Grade			●		
Terrain				●	
Navigation					●
Seriousness		●			

Assessment: a rough cliff-top coast walk with superb coastal scenery. The route involves no scrambling but is graded 3 to reflect its challenging nature.
Stack note: Talisker Bay and Stac an Fhucadair (The Fuller's Stack) on its south side are worth a short side trip. The stack has some impressive overhangs and a fine rock pavement beneath it, but it can be reached AT LOW TIDE ONLY.

North of Talisker Bay the cliffs of the Minginish coastline continue to Fiskavaig before they give way to the less severe scenery of Loch Bracadale. The walk from Talisker to Fiskavaig is shorter and less vertigo-inducing than its two neighbouring coast walks to the south (Routes 35 and 36), but the coastal scenery is almost equally spectacular. Moreover, a cross-country cart track makes the return journey easy.

Begin near Talisker at the end of the public road; go right through a farmyard and past a cottage to pick up the cart track to Fiskavaig. Follow the track to the first hairpin bend, then leave it and climb diagonally across the hillside on good sheep paths to reach the plateau above the bay. Follow the edge of the plateau until above the beach, where the cliffs begin. There is a stunning view from here around the cliff-lined north side of the bay to the 120m (400ft) headland of Rubha Cruinn, with a fine waterfall dropping from the plateau to the shore.

Rubha Cruinn is an excellent viewpoint for the cliffs of Biod Ruadh to the south (see Route 36), and then the coastline turns northwards away from Talisker Bay. There is no continuous shoreline route past McFarlane's Rock, so stay high over Sgurr Mor. Beyond Rubha Dubh a' Ghrianain a huge cauldron carved by the sea can be seen below on the shore. At the headland just beyond Geodh' an Eich Bhric a short diversion away from the cliff edge is required to outflank lines of small crags and a curiously deep-cut gorge carved out of the plateau by a small stream.

At Rubha nan Clach the coastline turns eastwards, leaving the open sea for the inner recesses of Loch Bracadale. The view over Loch Bracadale is stunning from any of the high vantage points around its

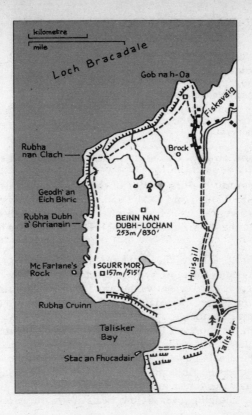

shores and Rubha nan Clach is no exception. The cliff top now becomes more complex and route-finding more interesting; small crags dot the moor and there is another substantial gorge to negotiate. The cliff edge is cut deeply by a number of streams and the easiest going will be found far back from the edge.

As Gob na h-Oa is approached a broch can be seen in a superb position crowning an eminence on the right. Continue to the headland above Gob na h-Oa for the fine view back along the coast to Rubha nan Clach, which includes numerous waterfalls dropping from the plateau. Beyond here stark cliffs give way to more serene scenery.

The route back to Talisker lies directly southwards. Contour onto the Fiskavaig road and walk up to a hairpin bend, then keep straight on along the excellent cart track that descends Huisgill to your starting point.

Route 38: **MACLEOD'S MAIDENS**

OS MAP: 23
Starting point: Loch Bharcasaig (GR: 252422)
Route type: return coast walk
Distance: 9 miles (14km)
Ascent: 390m (1,300ft)
Time: 5+ hours

	1	2	3	4	5
Grade	●				
Terrain	●				
Navigation			●		
Seriousness		●			

Assessment: an easy, classic coast walk to the highest sea stack on Skye.

Climbing note: the first ascent of the Mother stack was made in 1959 by I.S. Clough and J. McLean, who graded it a Severe rock climb. Reaching the stack first requires a spectacular abseil from the headland to the shore below, preferably leaving the rope in place.

The delightful walk to the three sea stacks known as MacLeod's Maidens is one of the most popular coast walks on Skye. For most of the way there is an excellently contoured path (boggy after rain), and the airy cliff top above the Maidens makes as dramatic an objective for a walk as any mountain top.

Begin on the shores of Loch Bracadale at Loch Bharcasaig bay, at the end of the Orbost road south of Dunvegan. The surfaced road ends at Orbost House, but a very rough road continues to the lochside and the bridge over the Abhainn Bharcasaig. From the bridge, follow a track through the forest and then a continuing path through new plantations, climbing over a low bealach to traverse high above Brandarsaig Bay.

Over the next rise lies the abandoned village of Idrigill and a level defile, from the near end of which a short detour leads to one of the most unusual coastal views on the island. Leave the path and climb up to an obvious clearing at the cliff edge half-way up the slopes of Ard Beag. The view from here back across Camas na h-Uamha bay includes a multitude of caves and stacks, but what makes it exceptional even by Skye standards are the remarkable double arches on the headland beyond, seen in profile one behind the other, the waters of Loch Bracadale surging through both.

The coastline between here and the Maidens has some spectacular caves, but unfortunately these can only be viewed by boat, so return to the path and continue through the defile. After passing more ruins, the path loses itself among sheep tracks, but if you keep heading straight across the moor, using the map as a guide, you should regain the coastline in the vicinity of the Maidens. If you reach a very large bay

CROFT BUNKHOUSE

**Pete Thomas
7 Portnalong
Isle of Skye
IV47 8SL
Tel/Fax 01478 640254**

Inexpensive self-contained Hostel - type Accommodation,
With Kitchen & Showers.
Open all Year.
Cycles for Hire.
Grid Ref: *NG348 353*

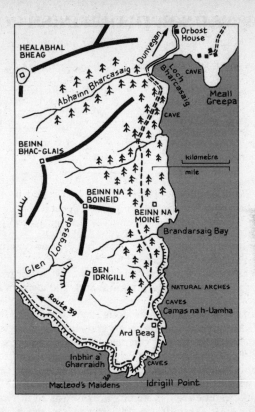

with cliffs rising westwards, this is the bay of Inbhir a' Gharraidh beyond the Maidens.

The crumbling cliff edge above the Maidens demands extreme caution. The setting is dramatic: the cairn on the cliff top is perched some 70m (230ft) above the crashing waves below, and the tallest Maiden (the Mother; 63m/207ft) stands close by; beyond stand her two daughters, one a dumpy pinnacle, the other seen from most angles as a thin rock blade. The best view of the Maidens is obtained from further round Inbhir a' Gharraidh, from where the three stacks appear in profile, the leaning summit block of the Mother resembling a head nodding to the two daughters. From this angle the Mother has a truly human appearance that has been likened to a statue of a seated Queen Victoria.

Return to Loch Bharcasaig by the outward route or continue to Ramasaig via Route 39.

Route 39: **THE SOUTH DUIRINISH COAST WALK**

OS MAP: 23
Starting point: Loch Bharcasaig
(end point Ramasaig)
(GR: 252422 (end point 165442))
Route type: one-way cliff-top
coast walk, add-on to Route 38
(distance/ascent/time include
Route 38 outward)
Distance: 14 miles (22km)
Ascent: 720m (2,350ft)
Time: 8¹/₂ hours (6 hours
from MacLeod's Maidens)

	1	2	3	4	5
Grade					●
Terrain		●			
Navigation					●
Seriousness				●	

Assessment: the finest cliff-top coast walk in the British Isles; awesome and breathtaking. The route involves no scrambling but is graded 5 to reflect its challenging nature.
Scenic note: the stunning coastal scenery at Glen Lorgasdal includes two stacks, a pinnacled arête, a natural arch and a waterfall.

The cliff-top walk that continues along the Duirinish coastline beyond MacLeod's Maidens is as vertiginous and exciting as they come – and note that the path marked on the map does not always exist.

Beyond the Maidens the route climbs around the cliff top above the bay of Inbhir a' Gharraidh, then descends slightly to reach the next headland, where there is a pinnacle low down on the cliff face. From here the route can be seen stretching northwards all the way to Lorgill Bay and beyond, the cliff top like a bowling green. The descent continues into Glen Lorgasdal to reach a wonderful stretch of coast-line that is studded with stacks and pinnacles (see note above).

Continue round the next headland to Glen Ollisdal and then round the next to the deep gorge of Glen Dibidal, through which the Dibidal River tumbles to the sea. The river is crossed above the gorge by taking a diagonal line down across the hillside. Beyond Glen Dibidal the coast becomes increasingly awesome, and great care is required on the crumbling cliff edge, which overhangs massive caves. Adding to the fearsomeness of the scene is the treacherous Black Skerry offshore.

After regaining the cliff top on the far side of Glen Dibidal, you reach the stream that drains Loch an Fhridhein, and from here a great archway cave can be seen cutting through the headland ahead. A fence leads on along the cliff edge above another large, deeply recessed cave (unviewable), and then a second archway cave comes into view, an enormous tunnel some 30m (100ft) long. On the next rise the cliffs reach 90m (300ft). Continuing along the cliff edge, descend to the

88

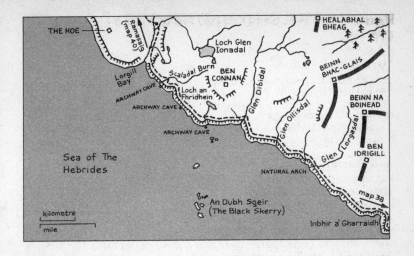

Scaladal Burn to view the largest cave of all, cutting deep into the cliff face ahead. Beneath your feet, but not viewable until you reach the far side of the Scaladal Burn, is a third archway cave, another huge tunnel some 15m (50ft) long.

The crossing of the gorge of the Scaladal Burn requires care: follow the edge of the gorge a short distance inland, until you find a sheep path that descends into the gorge above a waterfall and climbs back along a rock ledge on the far side. Follow the far side of the gorge down to the cliff edge for a view back to the third archway cave, then climb the steepest slope of the day to reach the vertiginous grassy summit of Biod Boidheach (GR 176408), where an iron fence-post provides security for the nervous.

From here the final descent of the day leads down to verdant Lorgill Bay. Beyond some ruined dwellings, pick up a path heading north-westwards onto the moor and join a cart track that leads to the road at Ramasaig.

Route 40: **MOONEN BAY HEIGHTS**

OS MAP: 23
Starting point Ramasaig
(GR: 165442)
Route type: circular cliff-top
coast walk
Distance: 8½ miles (14km)
Ascent: 590m (1,950ft)
Time: 5 hours

	1	2	3	4	5
Grade	●				
Terrain		●			
Navigation		●			
Seriousness	●				

Assessment: a mostly grassy walk over the three highest points on a line of great sea cliffs that front one of Skye's largest bays.
Twitchers' note: the huge coastal cliffs of north-west Skye are the best place on the island to view seabirds. The vertical cliffs surrounding Moonen Bay provide a safe home for colonies of fulmar, black guillemots and terns.

The west coast of Duirinish contains the highest sea cliffs on Skye. For mile after mile the cliffs present a more or less vertical wall unbroken by caves and stacks, and this gives the coastline a purity of line that is quite different from that of the south Duirinish coastline described in Routes 38 and 39. North of Lorgill Bay, the cliffs ring the large, crescent-shaped Moonen Bay. The road from Glendale to Ramasaig runs close to the cliff top and makes these magnificent cliffs readily accessible. There are three high points on the cliff top: the Hoe, Ramasaig Cliff and Waterstein Head. Each lies only a short distance across the moor from the roadside and can easily be climbed independently of the others; but a walk that clings to the cliff top and crosses all three makes a much finer outing, with excellent going and superb seaward views.

The Hoe stands immediately north of Lorgill Bay and is approached via the cart track from Ramasaig to Lorgill Bay described in Route 39. From Ramasaig, follow the track as far as its high point, then bear right over boggy ground to climb to the Hoe's mossy summit plateau, which is a wonderful lookout point for views both up the coastline to Ramasaig Cliff and Waterstein Head and down it to MacLeod's Maidens and the distant Cuillin. The summit itself is set well back from the cliff edge.

From here, turn northwards for a magnificent descent along the cliff top on beautiful short green turf to Ramasaig Bay. The headland of Hoe Rape half-way along makes a fine vantage point from which to view Ramasaig waterfall (GR 159438) and Loch Eishort waterfall (GR 155458) ahead, but beware if seabirds nesting on its northern face become aggressive.

North of Ramasaig Bay, keep to the cliff edge and climb steeply

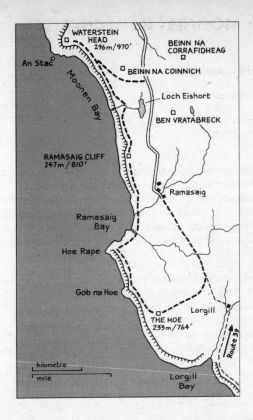

beside a fence to the top of Ramasaig Cliff. Between here and Waterstein Head the cliff edge becomes more indented and complex, especially at the point where the stream draining Loch Eishort tumbles over the cliff edge to form a waterfall; but navigation is easy if you keep to the right of the cliff-edge fence. The cliffs at Waterstein Head are the highest on Skye apart from Biod an Athair (see Route 41). The cliff face drops dramatically to An Stac and the crashing waves far below, but the fence stops you from getting too close to oblivion. The least eventful way back across the boggy moor from here to the Ramasaig road is to contour round the right-hand (southern) side of Beinn na Coinnich to reach the roadside north of Loch Eishort. A short walk then leads back to your starting point.

Route 41: **SKY CLIFF**

OS MAP: 23
Starting point: Galtrigill
(GR: 181546)
Route type: circular moor
and cliff-top coast walk
Distance: 4¹/₂ miles (7km)
Ascent: 270m (900ft)
Time: 3¹/₂ hours

	1	2	3	4	5
Grade	●				
Terrain				●	
Navigation			●		
Seriousness			●		

Assessment: an easy ascent to the highest sea cliff on Skye, followed by a rougher coast walk to a remarkable natural arch.

Manners note: below Galtrigill road end is the Manners Stone, a large flat stone on which you sit to find your manners. To locate it, descend past a ruined cottage with a prominent chimney, follow a fence down for 100 metres to a stile, and you will see the stone twenty metres to the left.

The extreme northern spur of the Duirinish peninsula between Loch Pooltiel and Loch Dunvegan forms a large subsidiary peninsula in its own right, whose entire western coastline is one continuous line of cliffs. This coastline makes a fine long walk, but as there is a road up the east side of the peninsula, the highest cliffs at Biod an Athair near Dunvegan Head can be reached more conveniently from the road end at Galtrigill.

From the road end the gently rising moor and seemingly inconsequential summit of Biod an Athair make the ascent appear deceptively simple; but the airy cliff edge demands great respect and the usual coast-walking precautions apply, especially if the recommended but much rougher continuation to the natural arch of Am Famhair (The Giant) is included. The best route across the heathery moor goes through the green fields above old Galtrigill village and along the banks of the Galtrigill Burn, veering right to reach the cliff edge and the summit. The best way to view the stupendous cliff face at the summit – and to appreciate its Gaelic name: Sky Cliff – is to lie down on the grass and peer over the edge at the miniature Atlantic breakers far below; but such is the scale of the face that its dimensions are hard to take in. To gain some perspective on the size of the cliff, continue northwards along the cliff top beyond the summit.

A good sheep path leads onwards along the cliff top towards Dunvegan Head but, as you progress, the cliff edge becomes less well delineated, the going becomes increasingly heathery and tough and the struggle to reach the undistinguished point of Dunvegan Head is hardly worthwhile. It is better at this point to aim straight across the moor to Am Famhair – an interesting exercise in navigation! Am

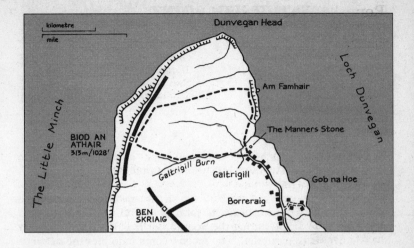

Famhair is one of the most remarkable natural arches on Skye, for it stands high and dry on the beach, completely unconnected to the cliff face and abandoned long ago by the sea, stranded like some prehistoric sculpture. To regain Galtrigill from Am Famhair it is best to take a direct line slightly away from the cliff edge in order to avoid the gorge of the Galtrigill Burn.

The coastline in the vicinity of Galtrigill is also worth exploring. At the south end of the beach at Galtrigill Bay is a prominent pipers' cave; pipers used to practise here in order not to incur the wrath of their neighbours. There is a Piping Centre at Borreraig. Expert and seaworthy scramblers who do not mind using limpets for footholds may find a careful sea-level exploration of the headland of Gob na Hoe more than exciting (but note that a slip would be awkward and that the complete girdle traverse involves rock climbing).

Route 42: **WATERNISH POINT**

OS MAP: 23
Starting point: Trumpan
(GR: 229616)
Route type: circular cliff-top
coast and moor walk
Distance: 9½ miles (15km)
Ascent: 220m (720ft)
Time: 7 hours

	1	2	3	4	5
Grade			●		
Terrain				●	
Navigation				●	
Seriousness			●		

Assessment: a rough and spacious walk around the loneliest peninsula on Skye. The route involves no scrambling but is graded 3 to reflect its challenging nature.

Historical note: on the track to Unish two prominent cairns are passed. The first is a memorial to John MacLeod of Waternish, who was killed here c1530 during the Second Battle of Waternish (against the MacDonalds, naturally). The second commemorates the death of his son Roderick MacLeod of Unish, who fell in the same battle.

The Waternish peninsula has neither the mountain scenery of Trotternish to the east, nor the coastal scenery of Duirinish to the west. It is, however, fine walking country, a remote, unfrequented and untamed land of wide horizons still echoing to the clash of claymores. The walk from Trumpan to Waternish Point is made easy by an excellent track, but the interesting continuation along the east coast (the Raven's Coastline) is a much more serious proposition, involving rough going on an airy cliff top.

The route begins at a right-angled bend in the road just north-east of Trumpan, and follows a Land Rover track up the peninsula to the ruined house at Unish. Short detours can be made along the way to view a number of sites of historical significance on the moor: two prominent cairns (see note above), Dun Borrafiach (one of the most beautifully constructed brochs on Skye) and Dun Gearymore (a more dilapidated broch but still worth exploring).

When the track bears right to the prominent ruins of Unish house, leave it and go left to reach the coastline at the pinnacled stump of An Camastac. The going along the cliff top from here to the unmanned lighthouse at Waternish Point is excellent, and there are fine coastal views. It was at Waternish Point that Prince Charlie and Flora MacDonald first touched Skye after their journey across the Little Minch from South Uist in 1746.

By far the easiest return route from the point is by the outward route, but keen coast walkers can make a rewarding circuit by continuing round the peninsula along the Raven's Coastline. Rugged cliffs and rough cliff-top terrain give the east side of the peninsula a

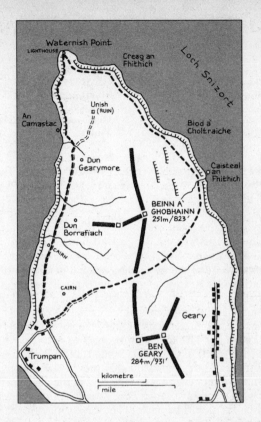

more serious air than the west side, but the coastal scenery is correspondingly more exciting. Heading eastwards along the cliff top to the headland of Creag an Fhithich (The Raven's Crag), then southwards to the headland of Biod a' Choltraiche (Razorbill Cliff), the going deteriorates; eventually it is best to stay away from the cliff edge, keeping to the moor until Caisteal an Fhithich (The Raven's Castle) comes into view. This fine grass-topped stack is almost as high as the cliff, to which it is connected by a short beach causeway; care is required at the cliff edge. The Crag and Castle are not named arbitrarily, as ravens do patrol this stretch of coastline.

To complete the round trip to Trumpan, leave the coast and cross the low backbone of the Waternish peninsula. Aim for the low point on the skyline between Beinn a' Ghobhainn and Ben Geary, then descend to pick up a grassy cart track at GR 240624, which takes you back to your starting point.

Route 43: **PROMONTORIES AND BAYS (EAST)**

Route 43a
OS MAP: 32
Starting point: the Braes
(GR: 525352)
Distance: 2 miles (3km)
Time: 1½+ hours

Route 43b
OS MAP: 23
Starting point: A855 near
Grealin (GR: 516625)
Distance: 2 miles (3km)
Time: 1½+ hours

Route 43c
OS MAP: 23
Starting point: Staffin Slipway
(GR: 494681)
Distance: 2 miles (3km)
Time: 1½+ hours

Route 43d
OS MAP: 23
Starting point: Duntulm Castle
(GR: 411741)
Distance: 5 miles (8km)
Time: 3+ hours

Route 43a: The Braes

On the seaward side of the small wing-shaped peninsula that juts out into the Narrows of Raasay opposite the Braes is a hidden stretch of coastline that harbours one of the most tantalising collections of secret caves, pinnacles and strange coastal formations on Skye.

The main area of interest lies south of the cove formed by the dog-leg in the coastline. The first feature reached is a cave that can be explored AT LOW TIDE ONLY; its 30m (100ft) long entrance canyon is flanked by 10m (30ft) high walls that prevent escape when the tide comes in. In the inlet beyond is a stack, and in the next inlet is an even larger cave whose entrance canyon can be reached by a scramble down a gully on the far side. The back of the cave splits into three or four arched caverns, in the deepest of which it is possible to stand upright some 20m (65ft) from the cave entrance.

Beyond the far bounding wall of the cave's entrance canyon is another canyon bridged by a natural arch, and just beyond here is the most remarkable formation of all: a 3m (10ft) long, eroded concertina of rock that stretches across a canyon like a fragile bridge. Please help its preservation (and yours!) by not attempting to cross it. Next comes a 3m (10ft) tall gendarme that adorns the end of a short ridge, beyond which the cliffs become smaller and provide bouldering problems galore.

Route 43b: Rubha Nam Brathairean

The narrow arête and exposed paths of Rubha nam Brathairean (Brothers' Point) make it one of the most exciting spots on the Trotternish coastline. To reach it, take the cart track opposite Glenview Inn, just north of the Grealin turn-off on the A855. After passing through a gate, turn immediately right on a path that curves down to a bay. The point lies further along the shore, guarded by a curious dun-like knoll. The ridge that leads out to the knoll narrows to a sharp arête that sports two gendarmes, giving a moderate but exposed scramble; easier sheep paths contour below the crest. A scramble over the knoll leads to green table-like pastures at the point beyond.

Route 43c: Staffin Slipway

On the south side of Staffin Bay a minor road cuts round the foot of cliffs to Staffin Slipway, where there are several features of interest. The most fascinating place to explore is a giant crazy pavement south of the slipway, reached by walking across flat marshy ground above the shore. The pavement is littered with huge boulders that have rolled down from the cliffs above, and in places the going is labyrinthine. A scramble round the boulders along the edge of the pavement above 5m (16ft) sea cliffs involves some interesting moves. Some of the cracks in the pavement are considerable, and it takes nerve to reach all the small promontories that jut out into the sea.

Route 43d: Rubha Hunish

Rubha Hunish is a worthy most northerly point on Skye. It is a long, grassy, crag-girt headland, lonely and breezy, fringed by beautiful stacks and almost completely cut off from the rest of the island by the 100m (330ft) cliffs of the appropriately named Meall Tuath (North Hill). There is only one route down through the cliffs, and even this is difficult to find without prior knowledge.

From Duntulm Castle, walk northwards along the shore of Tulm Bay, picking up a good sheep path on the grass just above the rocks. Approaching Rubha Voreven at the far end of the bay, shoreline rocks force you up the hillside, and at this point you should make directly for the coastguard lookout station at the summit of Meall Tuath.

There is no easy way round the cliffs that fringe the north side of the hill and bar the route to Rubha Hunish, and the only way down through them is from the dip between the summit and the south-west top. From the south-west side of this dip, a rocky path disappears behind a large boulder and zigzags down to the shore. The most interesting features of the headland lie hidden on its north-east side, where there are some fine sea cliffs, stacks and deep creeks to explore. Near the neck of the peninsula is a fine blade-shaped stack, and further out towards the point stands magnificent Bodha Hunish, a 30m (100ft) stack that is one of the most perfectly proportioned on Skye.

Route 44: **PROMONTORIES AND BAYS (WEST)**

Route 44a
OS MAP: 23
Starting point: Greshornish House (GR: 341541)
Distance: 4 miles (6km)
Time: 3 hours

Route 44b
OS MAP: 23 or 32
Starting point: near Ullinish (GR: 322374)
Distance: 3 miles (5km)
Time: 1¹/₂+ hours

Route 44c
OS MAP: 23
Starting point: near Roag (GR: 272433)
Distance: 1¹/₂ miles (2km)
Time: 1¹/₂+ hours

Route 44d
OS MAP: 23
Starting point: Neist Point road end (GR: 133478)
Distance: 2 miles (3km)
Time: 1¹/₂+ hours

Route 44a: Greshornish Point

The Greshornish peninsula is wild, remote and rarely visited, and the trip out to Greshornish Point makes a fine tramp, with an interesting dun and a number of stacks and caves to be viewed en route. The walk begins at Greshornish House Hotel, which is reached by a minor road that leaves the A850 Portree–Dunvegan road at Upperglen. Fifty metres beyond the hotel's entrance drive there is a sharp right-hand bend; the route begins here, on a cart track that goes through a gate on the left, bears right and forks. Take the left branch, which becomes a path across the neck of the peninsula to a small bay on the west coast.

From the bay, follow good sheep paths along the cliff top towards Greshornish Point. In the next bay are a number of caves and a 15m (50ft) tall finger of basalt; and in the bay beyond that stands a broader, grass-topped stack. The cliffs gradually increase in height and force the coast walker up to the high point of the peninsula at 97m (319ft). The cliffs then diminish in height towards Greshornish Point, where small crags fringe an area of lush green moss.

Turning southwards along the east coast, the next feature of interest is ruined Dun na h'Airde, which occupies a fine position on a rock promontory surrounded on three sides by 15m (50ft) high sea cliffs. Beyond here the east coast is mainly flat, and good going above the beach soon leads back to Greshornish House.

Route 44b: Oronsay

The ebb-tide island of Oronsay consists entirely of the finest stretch of greensward on Skye, sweeping up from the shore at the mainland end of the island to vertical 72m (236ft) cliffs overlooking Loch Bracadale. Beneath the high point is a wave-lashed skerry where two stacks hold out against the elements.

The island can be reached by a beach causeway AT LOW TIDE ONLY. Take either of the minor roads to Ullinish that leave the A863 just north of Struan. A few hundred metres east of Ullinish Lodge Hotel, take the road going south and park just before the last house. Follow a cart track past the house, then a path to Ullinish Point and the causeway.

Route 44c: Roag Island

At the southern end of Roag Island in Loch Bracadale, a large table-like rock bastion is separated from the rest of the island by a short stone causeway that almost turns it into another island in itself. The table is bounded by small crags that make it a delightful scramblers' playground.

To reach Roag Island, take the road to Roag village that leaves the A863 at Roskhill, then branch left to Ardroag and park on the landward side of the causeway that leads out to the island. Cross the causeway and follow the shoreline to reach the table. The most interesting formations are at the south-west point, where the deeply fissured tangle of rock is like giant, eroded crazy paving.

Route 44d: Neist Point

Neist Point juts out of Moonen Bay like a giant arm with rocky fingertips. The path to it begins at the car park at Neist Point road end and contours round the craggy lump of An t-Aigeach to reach Neist Point lighthouse. Between the lighthouse and the point a vast, three-dimensional rock pavement provides delightful scrambling.

Also from the road end, a path heads northwards above a two-tiered 120m (400ft) high cliff to a ruined coastguard lookout station, and from the edge of Oisgill Bay just beyond can be seen the stupendous 196m (645ft) high mural precipice of Biod Ban.

Also worth a visit:

Point of Sleat (OS map 32, GR 589008). A cart track and path lead to the lonely southern tip of Skye, where a lighthouse perches above honeycombed overhangs on a rocky headland.

Tarskavaig Bay and Point (OS map 32, GR 583097). A short Sleat coast walk leads from a sandy bay to a rock playground of labyrinthine creeks, canyons, beaches, rock shelves and other formations. Further along the shore is the cave of Uamh Tarskavaig, with its impressive entrance canyon.

Bearreraig Bay (OS map 23, GR 505525). Bearreraig Bay, at the foot of the Storr, is worth visiting for its waterfall, its fossils and its unique approach route: a 140m (450ft) descent of no less than 674 concrete steps beside a pulley-operated railway.

Route 45: **SEA STACKS AND WATERFALLS**

Route 45a
Starting point: Gillen
(GR: 268594 (OS map 23))
Distance: 4 miles (6km)
Time: 3+ hours

Route 45b
Starting point: near Lealt
(GR: 516605 (OS map 23))
Distance: 1 mile (1¹/₂ km)
Time: 1+ hours

Route 45c
Starting point: near Lealt
(GR: 515603 (OS map 23))
Distance: 3 miles (5km)
Time: 3+ hours

Route 45d
Starting point: near Balmacqueen
(GR: 450737 (OS map 23))
Distance: 1¹/₂ miles (2km)
Time: 1+ hours

Route 45e
Starting point: Port Gobhlaig
(GR: 437752 (OS map 23))
Distance: 1¹/₂ miles (2km)
Time: 1+ hours

Route 45a: Loch Losait Stacks
From Gillen road end in Waternish a track descends to the shore at Loch Losait (go left at the first fork and right at the second), and from here a boulder hop along the beach in either direction leads to an interesting stack. Westwards is 10m (35ft) high Stac Aros, whose far side yields an exposed, vegetated scramble to a guano-encrusted summit platform. Ten minutes further along the beach is a fine 30m (100ft) deep sea cave, accessible by a short scramble AT LOW TIDE ONLY.

Eastwards round a point is 15m (50ft) high Stac a' Bhothain, whose far side has a very impressive vertical cliff face. The stack is connected to the shore by a high neck that yields a vegetated scramble.

Route 45b: Lealt Waterfalls
The Lealt River in Trotternish drops steeply between the A855 roadside and the shoreline at Inver Tote to form some impressive waterfalls. From the car park on the north bank, go through the gate in the fence and turn right to reach the upper fall.

To view the lower fall, go along the edge of the gorge through a quarry and pick up a path on the right that meanders down the steep grassy hillside to Inver Tote. There are some old diatomite workings here, where diatomite from Loch Cuithir was dried and shipped (see Route 28). From Inver Tote, follow the near bank of the river back upstream to the impressive lower fall.

Route 45c: The Eaglais Bhreugach
The Eaglais Bhreugach (False Church) is an enormous boulder split by a vaulted archway. It stands on the Trotternish shore and can be

reached AT LOW TIDE ONLY by a bouldery shoreline walk from Inver Tote. To reach Inver Tote south side, go through the gate fifty metres south of the bridge over the Lealt River to an old road, then go right and immediately left through another gate to pick up a path that follows the gorge of the river down to the shoreline.

The Eaglais stands in a shallow bay 1 mile (1½km) along the beach; it is 12m (40ft) high and about 36m (120ft) round. Holing its centre is the huge arch that gives it its name, although according to tradition there is more to the name than mere appearance, for there are tales of pagan rites here, involving the roasting of cats. Beside the main arch is another smaller passageway and on the beach nearby is an isolated pinnacle some 5m (16ft) high called the Cubaid (Pulpit) of Satan. The scramble up the landward or seaward end of the Eaglais may tempt some, but the vegetated higher slopes are steep and dangerous.

It is worth continuing a short distance further along the beach to a 20m (65ft) long sea cave whose near wall is holed by another large arch; but beware the loose and waterlogged cliffs above, which are prone to rockfall. Return to Inver Tote while the tide is low.

Route 45d: The North-East Stacks

Between Creag na h-Eiginn and Port Gobhlaig, the Trotternish coastline bristles with outstanding sea stacks. The cliff top is easily reached by a short track that leaves the A855 coast road at a ruined building ½ mile (1km) south of the Balmacqueen turn-off, but great care is required at the cliff edge. Walking northwards along the cliff top, the first features of interest reached are the twin stacks of Stacan Gobhlach. Over the next high point, which is holed by a natural arch, stands the great needle of Stac Buidhe. Further along, just before the cliffs give out, a small inlet hides another huge stack whose summit is only about 6m (20ft) from the cliff top.

Route 45e: Stac Lachlainn

Sturdy Stac Lachlainn stands on the Trotternish shore north of Port Gobhlaig, reached by a minor road that leaves the A855 coast road just beyond the Connista turn-off (GR 434742). From Port Gobhlaig, follow the shoreline to the stack. Just before you reach it, there is a deep enclosed pool formed by a natural bridge through which the sea enters. On the seaward side of the stack is a natural arch that can only be seen from the shore.

A continuation along the coast leads to the desolate, featureless point of Rubha na h-Aiseag at the extreme north-eastern tip of Skye, where stack baggers should note the presence of Stac nam Meann on the west side of the bay (Lub) named after it.

Route 46: **SEA CAVES**

Route 46a
Starting point: Glasnakille
(GR: 537129 (OS map 32))
Distance: 1 mile (1½km)
Time: 1½+ hours

Route 46b
Starting point: Elgol
(GR: 516135 (OS map 32))
Distance: 2½ miles (4km)
Time: 2+ hours

Route 46c
Starting point: Ardmore
(GR: 284410 (OS map 23))
Distance: 1½ miles (2km)
Time: 1½+ hours

Route 46d
Starting point: Loch Bharcasaig
(GR: 257427 (OS map 23))
Distance: 1 mile (1½km)
Time: 1+ hours

Route 46e
Starting point: Bornesketaig
(GR: 376714 (OS map 23))
Distance: 1 mile (1½km)
Time: 1+ hours

Route 46a: Spar Cave

Renowned Spar Cave in Sleat is one of the natural wonders of Scotland, but reaching the entrance canyon requires scrambling along shoreline cliffs and over seaweed-encrusted rocks, and is possible AT LOW TIDE ONLY. The cave floor is muddy and steep, and a torch is required. Please, please do not remove or interfere with the calcite formations.

The route to the cave begins 150 metres south of the road junction in Glasnakille. Go down grassy slopes on the right of a ruined building to reach trees at the edge of shoreline cliffs. Turn left here on a path that winds down to a rocky inlet, then go left along the shoreline past a narrow flooded creek. The entrance to the cave lies round the next headland, and is reached by edging round rocky ledges and clambering over seaweed-encrusted rocks at the cliff foot. This section of the route is passable for only a couple of hours each side of low tide.

The entrance canyon is about 60m (200ft) long and up to 30m (100ft) high. The cave entrance itself lies at the landward end of the canyon, guarded by a 3m (10ft) high broken wall that was built in a futile attempt to prevent visitors from robbing the cave of its long pendant stalactites ('spars'). Beyond the wall the main passage goes left. It is muddy for some distance but then develops into a fantastic flowstone staircase some 50m (160ft) long, before descending again to a deep pool and the cave end.

Route 46b: Prince Charles's Cave

Suidhe Biorach (Pointed Seat) at the south-west tip of Strathaird sports some exciting cliff scenery and also the cave where Bonnie Prince Charlie spent his last hours on Skye in 1746. The headland's name derives from its supposed ability to make childless women fertile. From Elgol jetty, go southwards above the beach and pick up a sheep path that climbs onto the cliff top and follows the cliff edge all the way out to the point.

Prince Charles's Cave lies a short distance further along. Continue along the cliff top until you can descend to the shoreline, then return along the cliff foot. This is advisable AT LOW TIDE ONLY. The cave is 30m (100ft) long and is reached by a short, grassy scramble.

Route 46c: The Piper's Cave

The Piper's Cave at Harlosh Point is the longest sea cave on Skye; its exploration requires a scramble and a torch. The route to it begins at Ardmore on the Harlosh peninsula. From here, follow a grassy cart track to a gate in a fence, then continue southwards along the cliff top almost to Harlosh Point, until you reach a 10m (30ft) tall finger of basalt that rears up from the shore. From the cliff top opposite this pinnacle, an easy scramble leads down to the shore, and AT LOW TIDE ONLY it is possible to scramble left along the cliff foot to the cave entrance. Beyond the huge entrance arch, a 3m (10ft) square tube burrows into the hillside for 50m (160ft).

Route 46d: Meall Greepa

On the eastern shore of Loch Bharcasaig south of Orbost, a beautifully arched cavern some 40m (130ft) long by 10m (30ft) high tunnels through the headland of Meall Greepa to form the longest archway cave on Skye. To reach it from the lochside, follow a delightful rock platform out along the cliff foot. At one point the cliffs fall directly into the sea, but AT LOW TIDE ONLY this section can be crossed dry-shod on stepping stones to reach the mouth of the cave. Brave souls who do not fear the prospect of a wetting can cross the channel at the cave's entrance and scramble some distance up the centre of the channel on large blocks that have fallen from the roof; but a slip would be serious. Beyond the cave is a natural arch visible from certain angles during the approach walk but not reachable on foot.

Route 46e: The Uamh Oir

The Uamh Oir (Cave of Gold) is the closest Skye comes to having a cave to rival the wonders of Fingal's Cave on Staffa. Its name derives from its legendary use as a place to secrete valuables in times of trouble. The route to it begins at Bornesketaig in north-west Trotternish. From the road end, continue straight on along a track, then aim left to gain the cliff top. At a break in the cliffs, just before the cliff-top fence turns sharp right at the headland of Ru Bornesketaig, descend steep grass slopes to the shore. The Uamh Oir lies just round the corner on the right, its hexagonal basalt columns forming a perfect (but unreachable) rectangular entrance to the deep-water channel beyond. Beside the entrance is a crazy basalt pavement reminiscent of the Giant's Causeway in Antrim. After exploring the shoreline it is worth wandering along the cliff top around Ru Bornesketaig, until a magnificent needle stack and natural arch come into view.

Route 47: **HISTORICAL SKYE**

Route 47a
OS MAP: 32
Starting point: near Tokavaig
(GR: 601118)
Distance: 1 mile (1 1/2km)
Time: 1+ hours

Route 47b
OS MAP: 32
Starting point: Kilmarie House
(GR: 552173)
Distance: 1 1/2 miles (2km)
Time: 1+ hours

Route 47c
OS MAP: 23
Starting point: Totardor
(GR: 371395)
Distance: 6 miles (10km)
Time: 3+ hours

Route 47d
OS MAP: 23
Starting point: Cuidrach
(GR: 379595)
Distance: 1 1/2 miles (2km)
Time: 1+ hours

Route 47a: Dunscaith Castle

The dramatic ruined castle of Dunscaith in Sleat crowns a rocky head-land on the north side of Ob Gauscavaig Bay, and occupies a commanding position at the entrance to Loch Eishort. To reach it, take the track along the north side of the bay and then walk out along the shore.

The rock on which the castle stands rises 13m (40ft) from the sea and is surrounded by water on three sides. On the landward side it is separated from the mainland of Sleat by a ravine bridged by two arched walls, whose intervening bridge has long since collapsed. The gap across the ravine is only 2m (6ft) long, but the crossing requires edging along a narrow ledge beside either arched wall. Once across, a winding staircase leads to the now grassy summit of the rock. An alternative route to the top goes via an easy scramble from the beach to the left of the bridge.

The origins of Dunscaith are lost in the mists of time and steeped in legend. The legendary Irish warrior-hero Cuchullin is said to have stayed here, and the grass-topped rock on the shore below is Clach Luath (Luath's Stone), where he tied his hound Luath on return from the hunt.

Dunscaith is listed as an Ancient Monument, but it is not maintained and disintegrates a little more each year. In places the wall still reaches a height of 5m (16ft), but it cannot last forever. Long may it remain standing as a haunting reminder of times long past.

Route 47b: Dun Ringill

Dun Ringill (GR 562171) stands atop some curious sandstone cliffs on the east coast of Strathaird. The path to it begins at a gate in a fence just up the road from Kilmarie House. The dun is typical of many duns on Skye in that it crowns a rocky headland surrounded by sea cliffs on three sides, but it is untypical in its landward entrance, an 8m (25ft) passageway that is partly covered. Little else but the passageway remains. It is worth exploring a few hundred metres further along the shoreline beyond the dun, where brittle sandstone cliffs teeter precariously. There is a cave, and an arch whose supporting walls have been holed as if by giant punches. Beware falling rocks.

Route 47c: Tungadal Souterrain

The remarkable Tungadal Souterrain (GR 407401) is an 8 by 1m (25 by 3ft) square tunnel that runs under the earth like an ancient subway line. The bleak, boggy and obstacle-strewn approach route to it begins at Totardor road end east of Struan. A torch and wellies are recommended. Take the cart track up Glen Bracadale to Loch Duagrich, then cross the extremely marshy mouth of the loch to gain an overgrown path along the south-east shore.

To locate the souterrain from the fence at the head of the loch, walk along the foot of the hill slope on the right for about 150 metres, then climb to a clearing in the trees about thirty metres up; at the time of writing the site is marked by a wooden post.

Route 47d: Hugh's Castle

Hugh's Castle (GR 381583, Caisteal Uisdein on OS map) was built by Hugh MacDonald in the early seventeenth century and has a curious construction in that it contains no door. The walk to it begins at Cuidrach, south of Uig. When the road bears right at the bay of Poll na h-Ealaidh, go left along a Land Rover track and then keep straight on beside a fence to the high point of the moor directly ahead. The castle crowns some sea cliffs immediately beyond. It is a sturdy rectangular enclosure some 16m (52ft) long by 10m (32ft) wide, with walls up to 5m (16ft) high and 3m (10ft) thick. The easiest way in is to squeeze through a narrow chest-high window aperture. Inside are only nettles and fallen stones.

Also worth a visit:

Castle Camus (OS map 32, GR 670091). Caisteal Chamuis on OS map. Gaunt ruins perched at the cliff edge on a craggy Sleat headland, reached by a track and path on the north side of Knock Bay.

Dun Beag (OS map 23 or 32, GR 337385). The best preserved broch on Skye. Look for the roadside signpost on the A863 just north of the Ullinish turn-off near Struan.

Dun Fiadhairt (OS map 23, GR 239509). An interesting broch on a peninsula frequented by seals. From the corner of Loch Suardal north of Dunvegan, follow a farm track over a low hill to the peninsula's narrow isthmus.

Route 48: **DUN CAAN**

OS MAP: 24 or 32
Starting point: Raasay pier
(GR: 554342)
Route type: circular hill walk
Distance: 11 miles (18km)
Ascent: 530m (1,750ft)
Time: 7 hours

	1	2	3	4	5
Grade	●				
Terrain	●				
Navigation			●		
Seriousness	●				

Assessment: a spacious walk to the rugged and picturesque summit of Raasay's highest hill, whose lowly height belies its true stature.

'We mounted up to the top of Duncaan, where we sat down, ate cold mutton and bread and cheese and drank brandy and punch. Then we had a Highland song . . . then we danced a reel.'

JAMES BOSWELL describing his famous jig on Dun Caan in 1773 during his tour of the Hebrides with Samuel Johnson

Dun Caan is an exceptional little hill on several counts. It is the highest point on the Isle of Raasay and its isolated, distinctive castellated summit gives it superb views and the character and prominence of a much higher mountain. Surrounding the summit is an array of picturesque lochans, nestling at various levels on the hillside as though constructed by a landscape artist. Unlike Routes 49 and 50, Route 48 to the summit of Dun Caan can be completed without transport in a day between ferries from Skye, and the route begins at the pier.

From the pier, follow the road through Inverarish in the direction of North Fearns. Leave the road beside some ruined buildings at the forest edge for a forest track that goes straight on to a gate, then bear right on a path that climbs beside the forest fence to the Inverarish Burn.

The path crosses the burn, continues along its far bank and climbs across the moor to the top of a line of cliffs overlooking Loch na Mna. At the end of the cliffs another path is joined beside a curious lochan that has no outlet and is preserved only by a small rise in the surrounding land. In a dip below it lies another, larger loch (Loch na Meilich), and beyond here the path zigzags up steep grass slopes to the craggy summit of Dun Caan.

A return route via the ruined township of Hallaig on the east coast is recommended if time allows. Retrace your steps to the foot of the cliffs, then cut left to join a path along the moorland terrace between Loch na Mna and a band of cliffs on the east, passing an enormous fissure near the cliff edge further along. When the cliffs give out, descend to the lush pastures of Hallaig, whose forlorn ruins, on a shelf

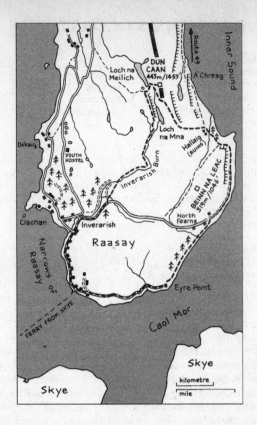

above a walled enclosure, remain a poignant symbol of the infamous Highland Clearances and are elegised in Sorley MacLean's emotive poem *Hallaig*.

The path out of Hallaig is difficult to distinguish at first among sheep paths; it will be found around the 100m (330ft) contour, about level with the cliff foot of Beinn na Leac. It contours along a shelf through natural woodland and rounds the foot of Beinn na Leac below a huge rock pillar, passing a memorial cairn displaying Sorley MacLean's poem in both Gaelic and English. The path eventually becomes a grassy cart track that provides a wonderful coast walk back to the road at North Fearns. At the second house in North Fearns, descend diagonally through fields on the left to the foot of a stream, then follow a path along the shoreline to Eyre Point and the road back to the ferry.

Route 49: **RAASAY EAST COAST**

OS MAP: 24
Starting point: North Fearns
(end point Brochel Castle)
(GR: 593360 (end point 583462))
Route type: one-way coast walk
Distance: 7 miles (11km)
Ascent: enough
Time: 5 hours

	1	2	3	4	5
Grade			●		
Terrain				●	
Navigation	●				
Seriousness				●	

Assessment: a 'walk on the wild side' of Raasay, following an adventurous old path along the island's remote eastern shoreline. The route involves no scrambling, but is graded 3 to reflect its challenging nature.

'The wide bright sea, the distant mountains of the mainland, and the long bold cliffs of Raasay . . . form landscapes not often equalled in singularity, or exceeded in beauty.'

JOHN MACCULLOCH
(*A Description of the Western Islands of Scotland,* 1819)

There are fewer wilder places to coast walk in the British Isles than the craggy, rarely visited east coast of Raasay, yet surprisingly there was once a good shoreline path here, built for deer stalking in the nineteenth century. The old path is now best described as 'sporting': landslides have carried sections of it away, while elsewhere it is sometimes so overgrown that rucksacks snag on trees and it is necessary to take to the shore. If the thought of such exploits brings a smile to your face, then one of the most adventurous shoreline routes in the country awaits its next challenger.

In the direction south to north, the route begins at the road end at North Fearns. The fine path from here to Hallaig is described in Route 48. Beyond Hallaig the path descends to the shoreline, continues along the edge of the beach and climbs again to surmount the shoreline cliff named A' Chreag. Note the ruins behind the cliff and elsewhere along the route, testifying to the number of people who formerly eked out a living on this now empty coast. Beyond A' Chreag the line of cliffs on the east side of Raasay gradually closes in and the going on the steep hillside beneath them becomes rougher, forcing you down onto the rocky shoreline in one place. At the next point there is a chaotic jumble of giant boulders and a stream crosses the path at the back of a deep cave-like recess, marking the onset of the toughest part of the route. Trees and thick vegetation crowd the steep hillside of Druim an

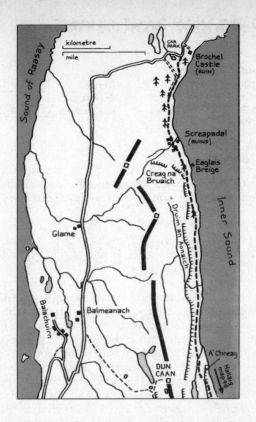

Aonaich and the path weaves a contorted route, its precise line dependent on the current state of landslides and fallen trees; again it takes to the shore when the going gets too tough.

At the point beyond this section is another jumble of huge boulders and beyond here the path improves to provide wonderful coast walking. The fantastic rock pillars of Creag na Bruaich erupt from the hillside above and on the shoreline at the next point is the Eaglais Breige (False Church), an enormous boulder whose name derives from its vaulted shape. The Eaglais Breige signals your arrival at the green fields of South and North Screapadal which, like Hallaig, are cleared townships whose forlorn ruins stand on a series of terraces that rise up the hillside. The path continues across the fields and enters forestry plantations, where it becomes a forest track parallel to the shoreline. When the track turns sharp left at a hairpin bend to end on Raasay's main road, keep right on a forest path that reaches the roadside further north, at a stile about 200 metres from Brochel Castle car park.

Route 50: **RAASAY NORTH END**

OS MAP: 24
Starting point: Arnish
(GR: 594480)
Route type: return moor
and coast walk
Distance: 10 miles (16km)
+ detours
Ascent: more than enough
Time: 6+ hours

	1	2	3	4	5
Grade	●				
Terrain		●			
Navigation	●				
Seriousness		●			

Assessment: a scenic walk on an historic path, leading through complex, picturesque terrain to the rarely visited northern tip of Raasay.

School note: when the north end was inhabited, children had to make the 6-mile (10km) return trip to the schoolhouse at Torran every day. Children coming from the tidal island of Fladda were regularly marooned on the mainland by the tide.

The rocky, indented coastline and emerald waters of northern Raasay give the landscape the character of a Greek island, and the walk to the northern tip is a wonderful excursion, full of interest. The route begins on a cart track that branches left at the end of the public road. Follow the track down around Loch Arnish to a fork at old Torran schoolhouse (the first building reached). Branch right here on a path that climbs out of the woods and round a cliff face (the Piper's Cliff) to reach a cairned junction; beyond this point the path can become boggy in places, although it may be improved in the future. Again take the right branch, which climbs to a high point of 150m (500ft) before undulating and winding along the knolly spine of the island to the old northern townships (marked as 'shielings' on the map). Beyond Lochan nan Ghrunnd, in the vicinity of a shepherd's hut, the path becomes very boggy and indistinct for a while; from the hut, look northwards to see a raised section that marks its continuation. The path ends at a small cove on Raasay's north coast.

Beyond the cove lies the rocky little island of Eilean Tigh, which can be reached AT LOW TIDE ONLY by a slippery causeway a short distance round to the left. The island consists entirely of one hill, which at 111m (365ft) makes a good viewpoint for the north end of Raasay and the island of Rona. To reach the very north tip of Raasay, walk out to Rubha nan Sgarbh on the far side of Eilean Tigh; it is probably easier to go over the hill than round it, as the bracken, bog, heather and crags that make up the island are awkward to negotiate. The Rubha is an unremarkable spot on the right of a small cove, but it makes a satisfying end to the route northwards.

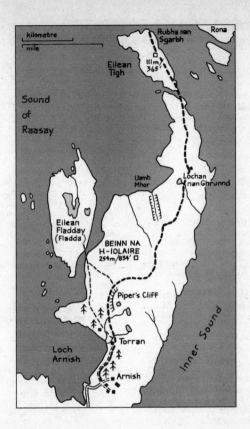

On the return journey to Arnish, two interesting detours can be made. On the ascent from Lochan nan Ghrunnd, when the path turns sharp left up a boggy defile, a rough scramble down the defile on the right will take you down to the shoreline cliffs and the Uamh Mhor (Big Cave). This is a false cave formed by a huge boulder jammed into the top of a gully; behind the boulder hangs another large needle-shaped rock, poised as though ready to prise the chockstone down onto your head.

The second (and easier) detour branches right at the cairned junction at the Piper's Cliff to visit the tidal island of Fladda; from the causeway over to the island a fine path goes southwards along the coast to rejoin the outward route at old Torran schoolhouse.

Glossary/Index

Note: entries are indexed by route number, not page.

112

Bealach nam Mulachag, Pass of the Hilly Place 24

Bealach nan Lice, *Byal*ach nan *Leek*a, Pass of the Slabs 4

Bealach Ollasgairte, *Byal*ach Olla*skarr*-stcha, poss. from Gaelic for Wool and Scree 31

Bealach Udal, *Byal*ach Udal, poss. Gloomy Pass 24

Bealach Uige, *Byal*ach Oo-iga, Pass of Uig 31

Bearreraig Bay 44

Beinn a' Mheadhoin, Ben a *Vay*-an, Middle Mountain 32

Beinn a' Ghobhainn, Ben a *Gho*-in, Mountain of the Blacksmith 42

Beinn an Dubhaich (Cave), Ben an *Doo*-ich, Mountain of Darkness 33

Beinn an Eoin, Ben an *Yai*-awn, Mountain of the Bird 35

Beinn Bheag, Ben Vake, Little Mountain 24

Beinn Bhreac, Ben *Vrai*-achk, Speckled Mountain 36

Beinn Bhuidhe, Ben *Voo*-ya, Yellow Mountain 25 (MacLeod's Tables), 32 (Suisnish)

Beinn Dearg Mhor (Bheag), Ben *Jerr*ak Voar (Vake), Big (Little) Red Mountain 20 (Glamaig), 23 (Beinn na Caillich)

Beinn Dearg Mheadhonach, Ben *Jerr*ak *Vay*-anach, Middle Red Mountain 20

Beinn Edra, Bain *Ett*era, The Between Mountain 31

Beinn na Boineid, Ben na *Bonn*aj, Bonnet Mountain 38

Beinn na Caillich, Ben na *Kyle*-yich, Mountain of the Old Woman 23 (Broadford), 24 (Kylerhea)

Beinn na Coinnich, Ben na *Coan*-yich, Mountain of the Moss 40

Beinn na h-Uamha, Bain na *Hoo*-aha, Mountain of the Cave 25

Beinn na Leac, Ben na Lyechk, Mountain of the Slab 48

Beinn na Moine, Ben na *Moan*-ya, Mountain of the Bog 38

Belig, Birch Tree Bark 22

Ben Aslak, Mountain of the Ridge or Hollow 24

Ben Cleat, Ben Clait, Mountain of the Cliff 17

Ben Dearg, Ben *Jerrak*, Red Mountain 31

Ben Geary, Ben Gyarry, Mountain of the Enclosure 42

Ben Leacach, Ben *Lyech*kach, Slabby Mountain 17

Ben Tianavaig, Ben *Tchee*anavaig, Mountain of the Sheltering Bay 26

Bidein an Fhithich, Beejan an *Ee*-ich, Raven Pinnacle 17

Bidein Druim nan Ramh, Beejan Dreem nan Rahv, Pinnacle of the Ridge of Oars 5, 18b

Biod a' Choltraiche, Beet a *Chol*trich-ya, Razorbill Cliff 42

Biod an Athair, Beet an *Ah*-hir, Sky Cliff 41

Biod Ban, Beet Bahn, White Cliff 44d

Biod Boidheach, Beet *Baw*-yach, Beautiful Cliff 39

Biod na Fionaich, Beet na Fee-*on*ich, Shaggy Cliff 36

Biod Ruadh, Beet *Roo*-a, Red Cliff 36

Bioda Buidhe, Beeta *Boo*-ya, Yellow Point 31

Bla Bheinn, also written Blaven, *Blah*-ven, Blue Mountain 13, 14

Bloody Stone, The 2, 15

Bodha Hunish, *Boe*-a Hoonish, Bear Reef 43d

Boreraig, *Borr*eraik, Castle Bay 32

Braes, The 26, 43a

Brochel, Rock Fort 49

Bruach na Frithe, *Broo*-ach na *Free*-ha, Hill or Edge of the Deer Forest or Wilderness 4, 5

C

Caisteal a' Garbh-choire, *Cash*-tyal a *Garr*av Chorra, Castle of the Rough Corrie 11, 12, 19c

Caisteal an Fhithich, *Cash*-tyal an *Ee*-ich, The Raven's Castle 42

Caisteal Chamuis, see Castle Camus

Caisteal Uisdein, see Hugh's Castle

Calaman Cave 32

Camas Ban, Cammas Bahn, White Bay 26

Camas Malag 32, 33

Camas Mor, Cammas Moar, Big Bay 46e

Camas na h-Uamha, Cammas na *Hoo*-aha, Bay of the Cave 38

Camasunary, in Gaelic Camas Fhionnairigh, Cammas *Ee*-oonary, Bay of the Fair Shieling 14, 17

Carn Liath, Carn *Lee*-a, Grey Cairn 27

Carn Mor, Big Cairn 34

Castle Camus, in Gaelic Caisteal Chamuis, *Cash*-tyal *Chamm*ish, Bay Castle 47

Choire a' Caise, Chorra a *Kash*a, Corrie of Steepness 13

Cioch, The, *Kee*-och, Breast 10

Clach Glas, Clach Glass, Grey Stone 13, 22

Clach Luath, Clach *Loo*-a, Luath's Stone 47a

Clach na Craoibhe Chaoruinn, Clach na *Cræ*-ya *Chæ*ran, Stone of the Rowan Tree 15

Clachan Gorma, Clachan *Gorr*ama, Blue Stones 36

Cleat, Clait, Cliff 31

Coir' a' Chaoruinn, Corra *Chæ*ran, Corrie of the Rowan 19b

Coir' a' Ghrunnda, Corra Ghrunnda, Floored Corrie 11, 12, 19b, 19c

Coir' a' Mhadaidh, Corra Vatty, Corrie of the Fox 5, 18b

Coir' a'Tairneilear, Corra *Tarn*yela, Corrie of the Thunderer 5

Coir' an Eich, Corran Yich, Horse Corrie 7

Coir' an Lochan, Corran Lochan, Corrie of the Lochan 19b

Coir' an t-Seasgaich, Corran *Tchays*-kich, Corrie of the Reeds 28

Coir' an Uaigneis, Corran Oo-*aig*-nis, Corrie of Solitude 18b

Coir'-uisg, Cor*ooshk*, Water Corrie 16, 17, 18, 19

Coire a' Bhasteir, Corra *Vash*-tyir, Corrie of the Executioner 3, 4

Coire a' Chruidh, Corra *Chroo*-y, Horseshoe Corrie 12

Coire Beag, Corra Bake, Little Corrie 12

Coire Faoin, Corrie *Fæ*-in, Empty Corrie 27

Coire Gorm, Corra *Gorr*am, Blue Corrie 33

Coire Lagan, Corra *Lah*kan, Corrie of the Hollow 9, 10

Coire na Banachdich, Corra na Banach-ich, Smallpox Corrie 8, 19a

Coire na Creiche, Corra na *Craich*-ya, Corrie of the Spoils 6

Coire nan Laogh, Corra nan Looh, Calf Corrie 12, 18 (Sgurr nan Eag), 21 (Marsco)

Coire Odhar, Corr *Oa*-ar, Dun-coloured Corrie 23

Coire Riabhach, Corra *Ree*-avach or *Ree*-ach, Brindled Corrie 1 (Sgurr nan Gillean), 16 (Coruisk)

Coire Scamadal, Corrie of the Short Valley 27

Coire Uaigneich, Corra Oo-*aig*nich, Remote Corrie 13

Coireachan Ruadha, *Corr*achan *Roo*-aha, Red Corries 19a

Creag an Fhithich, Craik an *Ee*-ich, The Raven's Crag 42

Creag Mhor, Craik Voar, Big Crag 34

Creag na Bruaich, Craik na *Broo*-ich, Crag of the Slope or Hill 49

Creag na h-Eiginn, Craik na *Haik*in, Crag of Distress or Violence 45d

Cubaid, Coobaj, Pulpit (of Satan) 45c

Cuillin, The, Coolin, poss. High Rocks (from the Norse *Kjælen*), Holly (from the Gaelic *Cuilion*, referring to the the serrated skyline) or Worthless (from the Celtic, referring to their agricultural potential). The name is unlikely to be derived from Prince Cuchullin of Antrim.

D/E/F

Druim an Aonaich, Dreem an *Œn*ich, Ridge of the Steep Place 49

Druim Hain, Dreem *Hah*-in, Ridge of Hinds 15, 16

Druim na Ruaige, Dreem na *Roo*-ig-ya, Ridge of the Hunt 20

Druim nan Ramh, Dreem nan Rahv, Ridge of Oars 16, 18b

Dun Beag, Dun Bake, Little Dun 47

Dun Borrafiach 42

Dun Caan 48

Dun Fiadhairt, Dun *Fee*-achursht, Dun of the Grassland 47

Dun Gearymore 42

Dun Kearstach, Dun *Kyar*stach, Dun of Justice 32

Dun na h'Airde, Dun na *Harj*a, Dun of the Point 44a

Dun Ringill, Dun of the Point of the Ravine 47b

Dunan Thearna Sgurr, *Doon*an *Hyarn*a Skoor, poss. Sloping Heap Peak 35

Dunscaith Castle, Dun*scaa*, poss. Dun of the Battle 47a

Eag Dubh, Aik Doo, Black Cleft 7

Eaglais Bhreugach, Ecklish *Vree*-agach, False Church 45c (Trotternish)

Eaglais Breige, Ecklish *Breeg*a, False Church 49 (Raasay)

Eas Mor, Aiss Moar, Big Waterfall 8

Eilean Reamhar, Ailen *Rav*ar, Fat Island 18a

Eilean Tigh, Ailen Ty, Island of the House 50

Faolainn, *Fæ*lin, Exposed Place by the Shore 36

Fionn Coire, Fyoon Corra, Fair Corrie 4

Fladda, Flat Island 50

G/H/I/J/K

Garbh-bheinn, *Garr*av Ven, Rough Mountain 22

Gars-bheinn, Garsh-ven, Echoing Mountain 12

Geodh' an Eich Bhric, Gyo-an Yich Vreechk, Cove of the Speckled Horse 37

Geodha Mor, *Gyo*-a Moar, Big Cove 39

Glac Mhor, Glachk Voar, Big Defile 18b

Glamaig, *Glah*-mak, Deep Gorge 20

Glen Brittle, Broad Dale 4, 5, 6, 7, 8, 9, 10, 11, 12, 18, 19, 34, 35

Glen Caladale, Cold Dale 36

Glen Dibidal, Deep Dale 39

Glen Lorgasdal 39

Glen Ollisdal 39

Glen Sligachan 2, 15, 16, 20, 21

Gob na h-Oa, Gope na *Hoe*-a, Beak of the Cave 37

Gob na Hoe, Gope na Hoe, Beak of the Hill or Spur 41

Great Stone Shoot, The 10

Greshornish Point, Point of the Promontory of the Pig 44a

Hallaig, Holy Bay 48, 49

Harlosh Point, Point of the Rock of the Fire 46c

Harta Corrie, Corrie of the Hart 2, 15

Hartaval, Hart Mountain 31

Healabhal Mhor (Bheag), *Hell*aval Voar (Vake), poss. Big (Little) Holy Mountain (after its altar-like appearance) 25

Hoe, The, The Hill or Spur 40

Hugh's Castle, in Gaelic Caisteal Uisdein, *Cash*-tyal Oosjin 47d

Inaccessible Pinnacle, The 9

Inbhir a' Gharraidh, Inyir a Gharry, Cove of the Walled Enclosure 38

Kyle Akin, *Ak*in, Strait of Acunn (a legendary Fienne) 24

Kyle Rhea, Ray, Strait of Readh, Acunn's brother 24

L/M/N/O

Leac nan Fionn, Lyechk nan *Fee*-on, Fingal's Tombstone 30

Lealt Waterfalls, Leth-allt, Lai-*owlt*, Half-stream 45b

Loch a' Choire Riabhaich, Loch a Chorra *Ree*-avich, Loch of the Brindled Corrie 16

Loch an Fhir-bhallaich, Loch an Eer *Vall*ich, Loch of the Spotted Man 9, 10

Loch an Leth-uillt, Loch an Lai Oolt, Loch of the Half Stream 35

Loch Bharcasaig, Loch *Var*kasaig, Castle Bay 38, 46d

Loch Bracadale, Loch of the Meeting of Townships 37, 38, 44b, 44c, 46c

Loch Brittle 34, 35

Loch Coruisk 16, 17, 18, 19

Loch Cuithir, Loch *Coo*-hir, Loch of the Cattle Fold or Rocky Area 28, 45d

Loch Eishort, Loch of the Icy Bay or Fjord 32, 47a

Loch Eynort, Loch of the Isthmus 36

Loch Hasco, Loch of the High Place 30

Loch Langaig, Loch of the Long Bay 30

Loch Leathan, Loch *Lyeh*-han, Broad Loch 27

Loch Lonachan, Marshy Loch 32

Loch Losait, Loch *Loss*aitch, Loch of the Small Stream or Hollow 45a

Loch na Cuilce, Loch na *Cool*-kya, Loch of Reeds 17

Loch na h-Airde, Loch na *Har*ja, Loch of the Point 34

Loch na Meilich, Loch na Mellich, Loch of the Bleating of Sheep 48

Loch na Mna, Loch na Mraa, Loch of the Wife or Woman 48

Loch na Sguabaidh, Loch na *Skoo*-aby, Sweeping Loch 22

Loch Scavaig 15, 16, 17

Loch Slapin, Muddy or Sluggish Loch 13, 22, 32, 33

Lochan nan Ghrunnd, Floored Lochan or Lochan of the Ground 50

Lorgill Bay, Bay of the Glen of the Deer Cry 39

Lota Corrie, High Corrie 2

MacLeod's Tables 25

Mam a' Phobuill, Mahm a *Foe*-pill, People's Moor 21

Manners Stone, The 41

Maoladh Mor, *Mœl*a Moar, Big Bare Hill 29

Marsco, Sea-gull Rock 21

Meall Greepa, Mell Greepa, Precipice Hill 46d

Meall na Cuilce, Mell na *Kool*ka, Hill of the Reeds 16

Meall na Suiramach, Mell na *Soor*amach, Maiden Hill 29, 31

Meall Tuath, Mell *Too*-a, North Hill 43d

Moonen Bay, named after the Ossianic hero Munan 40, 44d

Nead na h-Iolaire, Nyed na *Hill*era, Eagle's Nest 1

Neist Point (originally An Eist, An Eesht, The Horse) 44d

Oisgill Bay 44d

Old Man of Storr, The 27

Oronsay 44b

P/Q/R

Pein a' Chleibh, Pane a Chlee, Mountain of the Chest 31

Pinnacle Basin 31

Piper's Cave, The 46c

Point of Sleat 44

Port an Luig Mhoir, Porst an *Loo*-ik Voar, Harbour of the Big Hollow 46b

Port Gobhlaig, Porst Goalaig, Forked Harbour 45d

Preshal More (Beg), Big (Little) Preshal 37

115

Prince Charles's Cave 46b

Quiraing, The, Kwi-rang, The Round Cattle Fold (ie the Table) 29, 31

Ramasaig Cliff, Cliff of the Raven's Bay 40

Roag Island 44c

Ru Bornesketaig, Point of the Low Headland 46c

Ruadh Stac, *Roo*-a Stachk, Red Stack 21

Rubh' an Dunain, Roo-an Doonan, Headland of the Dun 34

Rubha Ban, *Roo*-a Bahn, White Headland 17

Rubha Buidhe, *Roo*-a *Boo*-ya, Yellow Headland 17

Rubha Cruinn, *Roo*-a *Croo*-in, Round Headland 37

Rubha Dubh a' Ghrianain, *Roo*-a Doo a *Gree*-anin, The Black Headland of the Sunny Place 37

Rubha Hunish, *Roo*-a Hoonish, Bear Point 43d

Rubha na h-Airighe Baine, *Roo*-a na Harry *Ban*-ya, Point of the White Shieling 17

Rubha na h-Aiseag, *Roo*-a na *Hash*ik, Ferry Point 45e

Rubha na Maighdeanan, *Roo*-a na *Ma*-ijanan, The Maidens' Headland 38

Rubha nam Brathairean, *Roo*-a nam *Bra*-huren, Brothers' Point 43b

Rubha nan Clach, *Roo*-a nan Clach, Stony Headland 37

Rubha nan Sgarbh, *Roo*-a nan *Skarr*av, Cormorant Point 50

Rubha Suisnish, Suisnish Point 32

S

Sanctuary, The 27

Screapadal, Rough Dale 49

Sgumain Stone Shoot, The 10

Sgurr a' Bhasteir, Skoor a *Vash*-tyir, Peak of the Executioner 4

Sgurr a' Choire Bhig, Skoor a Chorra Veek, Peak of the Little Corrie 12

Sgurr a' Fionn Choire, Skoor a Fyoon Chorra, Peak of the Fair Corrie 4

Sgurr a' Ghreadaidh, Skoor a Gretta, Peak of the Clear Waters 7

Sgurr a' Mhadaidh Ruaidh, Skoor a *Vah*ty *Roo*-y, Fox Peak 28, 31

Sgurr a' Mhadaidh, Skoor a *Vah*ty, Peak of the Foxes 7

Sgurr Alasdair, Skoor Alastir, Alexander's Peak (after Alexander Nicolson, who first climbed it in 1873) 10

Sgurr an Duine, Skoor an *Doon*a, Peak of the Person 35

Sgurr an Fheadain, Skoor an *Ait*enn, Peak of the Waterpipe 6

Sgurr Beag, Skoor Bake, Little Peak 2 (Sgurr nan Gillean), 36 (Loch Eynort)

Sgurr Buidhe, Skoor *Boo*-ya, Yellow Peak 36

Sgurr Coir' an Lochain, Skoor Corran Lochin, Peak of the Corrie of the Lochan 19a

Sgurr Dearg, Skoor *Jerr*ak, Red Peak 9

Sgurr Dubh Mor, Skoor Doo Moar, Big Black Peak 11

Sgurr Dubh na Da Bheinn, Skoor *Doo* na *Dah Vain*, Black Peak of the Two Mountains 11

Sgurr Eadar Da Choire, *Skoor* Aitar *Dah Chorra*, Peak Between Two Corries 7

Sgurr Hain, Skoor *Hah*-in, Peak of Hinds 15

Sgurr Mhairi, Skoor Varry, Mary's Peak (after a young local girl who perished on the mountain while looking for a stray cow) 20

Sgurr Mhic Choinnich, Skoor Veechk *Choan*-yich, Mackenzie's Peak (after John Mackenzie, the famous nineteenth-century Skye guide) 9

Sgurr Mor, Skoor Moar, Big Peak 31 (Trotternish), 37 (Talisker)

Sgurr na Banachdich, Skoor na *Banach*-ich, Smallpox Peak 7, 8

Sgurr na Bhairnich, Skoor na Varnich, Limpet Peak 5

Sgurr na Coinnich, Skoor na *Coan*-yich, Peak of the Moss 24

Sgurr na h-Uamha, Skoor na *Hoo*-aha, Peak of the Cave 2

Sgurr na Stri, Skoor na Stri, Peak of Strife 15

Sgurr nam Boc, Skoor nam Bochk, Peak of the He-goat or Roe-buck 35

Sgurr nam Fiadh, Skoor nam *Fee*-a, Deer Peak 36

Sgurr nan Bairnich, Skoor nan Barnich, Limpet Peak 35

Sgurr nan Each, Skoor nan Yech, Peak of the Horses 22

Sgurr nan Eag, Skoor nan Aik, Notched Peak 12

Sgurr nan Gillean, Skoor nan *Geel*-yan, Peak of the Gullies 1, 2

Sgurr nan Gobhar, Skoor nan *Goa*-ar, Goat Peak 8

Sgurr Sgumain, Skoor Skooman, Mound or Stack Peak 10

Sgurr Thearlaich, Skoor *Hyar*lach, Charles's Peak (after Charles Pilkington, who was the first to climb the Inaccessible Pinnacle, with his brother Lawrence, in 1880) 10

Sgurr Thormaid, Skoor *Hurr*amitch,

Warner Books now offers an exciting range of quality titles by both established and new authors. All of the books in this series are available from:

Little, Brown and Company (UK),
P.O. Box 11,
Falmouth,
Cornwall TR10 9EN.

Fax No: 01326 317444.
Telephone No: 01326 372400
E-mail: books@barni.avel.co.uk

Payments can be made as follows: cheque, postal order (payable to Little, Brown and Company) or by credit cards, Visa/Access. Do not send cash or currency. UK customers and B.F.P.O. please allow £1.00 for postage and packing for the first book, plus 50p for the second book, plus 30p for each additional book up to a maximum charge of £3.00 (7 books plus).

Overseas customers including Ireland, please allow £2.00 for the first book plus £1.00 for the second book, plus 50p for each additional book.

NAME (Block Letters) ....

....

ADDRESS ....

....

....

☐ I enclose my remittance for ....

☐ I wish to pay by Access/Visa Card

Number ☐☐☐☐☐☐☐☐☐☐☐☐☐☐☐☐

Card Expiry Date ☐☐☐☐